A READER'S

Many times in this book of Carole's Story, Barbara Whitfield talks about the depth of friendship, love and caring that she and Carole shared despite the horrible truths that lie in the depths of their own lives— She writes:

"It was deep because we placed no limits on it. We struggled with one of the deepest and darkest forms of wounding that the human Soul must bear. It was certainly our 'Dark Night of the Soul.' The pain of our struggle transformed our lives and helped us to realize some of the highest spiritual attainment that one can achieve in this earthly life.

"We did that by sharing all of our inner life, our darkness and our Souls' emerging light. We shared all of our pain and joy and, as a result, we became the deepest of confidantes, safe and supportive for each other. Our wounding and our spirituality were a lot alike. We were mirrors of each other in many if not all ways."

In the midst of their struggle with soul-destroying abuses, Charles Whitfield MD, author of the best selling *Healing the Child Within* and ten other books on recovery from childhood trauma, added his deep insight, talent and skills. In fact, both Whitfields brought to bear their own experiences in writings on healing from trauma and natural spirituality.

As the story unfolds, we, the readers, discover that the power of healing, when we are among a group of safe and supportive people, is far greater than the sum of all that we carry as individuals.

As we read, we stand by Carole who immersed herself in the painful truths of being a victim of incest perpetrated by her father and worked her own path to healing. We stand with her as she turned her transformative experience into her powerful art form —a documentary called "*Our Natural Soul.*"

Barbara continues:
"After many years, I felt that I must honor Carole --and all victims of abuse-- by telling our deeply human story of sadness and pain, of struggles through our Souls' darkness and eventually emerging into the light. Writing this book is my art form. This book is not about succumbing to our pain as a victim. Rather, it is a book about the sometimes long and arduous path that we must travel in order to heal our internal wounds and release ourselves from suffering." We read here the detailed story of a person who chooses what I refer to as "The Path of Most Resistance," the path that transforms us from

a wounded victim of abuse to a survivor and then on to becoming a thriver, living with more peace and even joy.

From my own experience, I understand that we step onto this "path" when we awaken to the truth that we were, in fact, a victim of someone's abuse and then choose to climb upward, calling upon our deep inner resources and that of safe others so that we can learn how to let go of our suffering. On this path, we learn to take responsibility for our own recovery. We make a gradual climb out of the morass of our pain and compulsions and acknowledge that we are survivors of what are often soul-killing abuses. With the encouragement of safe others, we press on until we become free. We transform our prior suffering and fragmentation into strength and wholeness. We begin to thrive in a world that once held nothing but fear, shame, confusion and other self-defeating influences. I've discovered that life's pains don't go away when we walk this path, but we can learn to let go of our suffering. Paradoxically, our suffering decreases when we accept or, *lean into* our pain and we don't try to fight or alter it.

This is not an easy book to read. It contains real-life pain, sadness and loss. Some of us have suffered like Carole did --and worse-- yet in reading this book – we discover healing. There is help here. And most importantly, *there is <u>hope</u> within these pages* for anyone who has been severely and repeatedly traumatized, abused and/or neglected in childhood. Whitfield quotes from Carole's documentary: "*The thunderstorms are just as beautiful as a sunny day. And so is life!*"

Carole's story is beautiful and contains thunderstorms and sunny days -- and they are all framed with the love the author and Carole shared. In reading this story, Carole's discoveries and selfless love may help the reader to heal and to once again find those beautiful, sunny days.

I am deeply grateful to Barbara and Charles who had the courage to write this book for the benefit of all of us who are survivors of childhood trauma, neglect and abuse. They have patiently and kindly stood beside me as I have come to accept my own past and work though my own suffering, grief and losses. They have helped me along the sometimes dark path that leads us from being a victim, through being a survivor and then onto something I could never have conceived of becoming: *a thriver* in life.

Barbara always likes to say, *"In the end, only kindness matters."* I have found the kindness she speaks of and it is my hope that, as you read this book, you will find all of the kindness and healing that belongs to you.

Donald Brennan   Atlanta, Georgia January, 2011

ON THE COVER

The cover art layout of this book is simple but contains several messages. It indicates a pattern of growth that we may experience as we move from being the victim of someone's abuse, to embracing our survivor skills that we learned. Eventually, we become free and whole, and we discover that we are lovable, loving and loved.

It may express what many of us feel after growing up in households where abuse, neglect, abandonment, and violence were prevalent. When we are the victim of someone else's behavior, we don't feel real; our life is faded into a background of shame, fear and pain. Our *Child Within*, or our *True Self* goes into hiding and our ego begins to protect us.

When we find help we begin learning the process that shifts our focus away from the cold comfort of our "victim stance" and we come to understand and embrace our survivor skills as the necessary tools that we developed in order to survive during our abuse and trauma. We learn to grieve our ungrieved losses, sadness, shame and fear with safe and supportive people. We begin feeling that we are *in fact* a real person and that we do not have to earn the right to be alive, whole, and loved. We begin to stand on our own.

As we press forward, we move beyond our survival skills and our protective ego and we begin living in this world as fully human, unique, worthy of love and respect. Our life takes on a clarity that we may never have experienced before. We gain back our dignity and our life.

In short, we begin to *thrive* where we only thought we could merely exist. Life becomes worth living.

—DB

Barbara Harris Whitfield

AUTHOR OF: *THE NATURAL SOUL, SPIRITUAL AWAKENINGS,*
FULL-CIRCLE, FINAL PASSAGE AND THE POWER OF HUMILITY

Please note: *The names in this book have been changed*
to protect the innocent and to disarm the guilty.

𝔐𝔥P
muse house press

BEYOND THE TRAUMA,

BEYOND THE PAIN,

BEYOND THE SCARS,

WE ARE SOUL.

WE ARE WHOLE.

WE ARE GOD'S CHILDREN

--BHW

ABOUT THIS BOOK

This is a true story for anyone touched by childhood trauma, abuse or neglect-- for those victims who have been preyed upon, suffered and dreamed of climbing out-- of disconnecting from the darkness holding them captive.

Carole's Story is a beacon to awaken and reconnect with our wholeness --to our Soul-- or whatever we choose to call that quietly knowable part of us that is connected to Spirit and ultimately to our God source.

To begin our journey of healing, we can use the table on the next two pages to discover what the landscape of the journey "looks like."

There is *a way out* of suffering and a way to heal the wounds that we have suffered. We can, in fact, choose to transform our lives and to move from victim to survivor and on to becoming a *thriver*.

Important note:

This story is heart-wrenching. However, it contains many gifts, too. If you feel triggered, or greatly upset, please stop reading and consult a therapist trained in childhood trauma or co-dependence. Share with them what is coming up for you.

This book does not replace the counsel of a trained health professional.

—BHW & DB

PROGRESSION FROM VICTIM TO SURVIVOR AND THRIVER

Victim	Survivor	Thriver
Doesn't deserve nice things or trying for the "good life."	Struggling for Reasons & Chance to Heal	Gratitude for everything in life
Low self-esteem/ shame/unworthy	Sees self as wounded & healing	Sees self as an overflowing miracle
Hyper-vigilant	Using tools to learn to relax	Able to experience peace
Alone	Seeking help	Oneness
Feels Selfish	Deserves to seek help	Proud of healthy self-caring
Damaged	Naming what happened	Was wounded & now healing
Confusion and Numbness	Learning to grieve, grieving past ungrieved trauma	Mostly content, & can grieve present losses easily
Overwhelmed by the Past	Naming and grieving what happened	Living in the present
Hopeless	Hopeful	Faith in self & life
Uses Outer World to Hide from Self	Stays with emotional pain	Understands that emotional pain will pass & brings new insights
Hides their story	Not afraid to tell their story to safe people	Transforms to Hero's Journey
Believes everyone else is better, stronger, less damaged	Comes out of hiding to hear others & have compassion for them and eventually self	Lives with an open heart for self & others
Needs People & Chemicals to Believe They are All Right	Glimpses of self-assurance & fun without others	Feels authentic & connected, Whole

Victim	Survivor	Thriver
Often Wounded by Unsafe Others	Learning how to protect self by "share-check-share"	Protects self from unsafe others
Places Own Needs Last	Learning healthy needs (See the books: *Healing the Child Within & Gift to Myself*)	Places self first realizing that is *the only* way to function & eventually help others
Creates One Drama After Another	Sees patterns	Creates peace
Believes Suffering is the Human Condition	Feeling some relief, knows they need to continue in recovery	Finds joy in peace
Serious All the Time	Beginning to laugh	Seeing humor in life
Uses Inappropriate Humor, Including Teasing	Feels associated painful feelings instead	Uses healthy humor
Uncomfortable, Numb, or Angry Around Toxic People	Increased awareness of pain and dynamics	Healthy boundaries around toxic people including relatives
Lives in the Past	Aware of patterns	Lives in the Now
Angry At Religion	Understanding the difference between religion & personal spirituality	Enjoys personal relationship with the God of their understanding
Suspicious of Therapist	Sees therapist as guide during projections	Sees reality as their projection & owns it
"Depression"	Movement of feelings	Aliveness

ꟿꞍꝜ
muse house press

ISBN: 978-1-935827-11-5

Trade Paperback
© Copyright 2011 Barbara Harris Whitfield
All Rights reserved

Request for information and rights should be addressed to:
Muse House Press

Find us on the Internet at:
www.MuseHousePress.com

Muse House Press is an imprint of Muse House Press, Inc.

Find Barbara on the Internet at:
www.BarbaraWhitfield.com
www.Barbara-Whitfield.Blogspot.com

Cover Design: Donald Brennan / YakRider Media
Interior Composition: Donald Brennan / YakRider Media

Printed in the United States of America

DEDICATION

For Carole

And for all survivors of childhood trauma, abuse and neglect
—Carole wanted you to know her story.

ACKNOWLEDGEMENTS

Special thanks to Vincent J. Felitti, MD and Robert F. Anda, MD, MS (Co-Principal Investigators, Adverse Childhood Experiences (ACE) Study) for the great work they have done on this study and for permission to allow us to summarize their results from their chapter in *The Hidden Epidemic: The Impact of Early Life Trauma on Health and Disease* (R. Lanius & E. Vermetten editors.)

Charles L Whitfield, MD is a collaborator and co-author on the ACE Study and contributed to eight of the published papers in peer reviewed scientific journals. His foreword and his summary at the end give this book and Carole's story credibility.

I want to give a big thanks and my gratitude to Eileen King of *Justice for Children* and Sherry Quirk of *First Star* in Washington, DC who are working to raise the consciousness of our society about the failure of our governmental agencies to protect victims of child abuse, to provide legal advocacy for abused children and to develop and implement collaborative solutions to enhance the quality of life for these children. Eileen and Sherry give tirelessly of themselves to further the cause of protecting our children and keep all of us in this field connected. Eileen introduced us to Carole and Alex. Because of this introduction, our lives were and always will be remarkably affected as you will read. Eileen also introduced us to Rob Anda who then invited Charlie to join his ACE Study team of researchers and writers on the short and long term health and functioning effects of childhood trauma. The ACE study was of great interest to Carole and she said many times that she could be the "poster child" for it. As mentioned above, there is an appendix at the end of this book summarizing this important study and its conclusions.

Of course, my thanks and acknowledgement also goes to Carole's husband who in this book we have called Alex to protect his privacy. I also want to thank his family for their caring and companionship during this true story.

My gratitude and deep thanks go to Donald Brennan for his talent and creativity in designing this book and getting it ready for publishing. Thanks to Nan Britt, as well, for her fine copy editing. Both Donald and Nan offered me the encouragement and enthusiasm that I needed to bring this story to press.

I also want to acknowledge the patients and psychotherapy group members that Charlie and I have worked with over the last 15 years. They have demonstrated the courage to face their pain by feeling compassion for one another and eventually learning to have compassion for themselves. With them as role models I have found the courage to release this book.

I would like to thank Lindsay Jenkins at Lightning Source for her patience and gracious help in publishing this book whose time has come.

Last, and most amazing, I want to thank Spirit (God, Goddess, All-That-Is) for the guidance that has accompanied every moment of the creation of *Victim to Survivor and Thriver: Carole's Story.*

TABLE OF CONTENTS

FOREWORD

Charles L. Whitfield, M.D.

Carole was a dear friend of mine. Although our relationship here on earth lasted only three years—it was an intense time. Carole's story of her own childhood trauma mirrored the research and clinical work I was doing at the time and continue to do. As I often explained to Carole: her current medical conditions were painful proof of the aftereffects of her trauma from her childhood. Her list of maladies often reflected the information in my writing (e.g., *Memory and Abuse* 1995, *The Truth about Depression*, 2003, *The Truth about Mental Illness*, 2004, *You May not Be Mentally Ill*, 2011).

In 1998 Carole cheered as I joined a team of researchers at the Centers for Disease Control and Prevention (CDC) on a project called the Adverse Childhood Experiences (ACE) Study. Carole celebrated. What she had known and lived her entire life of 34 years was finally being validated in a large CDC study that was being well received by several prestigious medical journals. She often asked me what was happening with the ACE study. She said that she could be the "poster child" for what we in this new field of trauma psychology were reporting. Carole's story illustrates beautifully but painfully the truth of our new reports. (See Appendix for list of the ten kinds of repeated childhood trauma which the study team called ACEs. Carole experienced seven of the ten.)

In a nutshell, here is what we now know. Trauma is any event, usually a non-ordinary one, that harms the body, self, or spirit. It covers a broad range of hurtful experiences, including traumas that involve the physical, sexual, mental or emotional realms of our being (van der Kolk & Fisler 1995; Whitfield 1995; 2010).

Until recently, medicine has focused mostly on physical trauma, which many physicians, nurses and allied health professionals think is the only kind. But the field of trauma psychology has been developing for the past century. We first learned of it from Janet, Brauer, and Freud, and later from numerous observers of combat trauma (Whitfield 1995, 1998, 2010). More recently, we have begun to fine-tune our knowledge by observing different kinds of trauma, from physical violence to child sexual abuse to growing up in an alcoholic or other dysfunctional family (Herman 1992; van der Kolk & Fisler 1995).

If the trauma is accepted as real and the victim or survivor's experience is validated and its expression supported, as happened in the Oklahoma City bombing incident, and the 9-11 attack, its short-term effects, also known as acute traumatic stress (American Psychiatric Association 1994), can be expressed, processed, ameliorated, or "metabolized" in a healthy way so that eventually few or no lasting detrimental effects remain (Herman 1992). However, if the reality of the traumatic experience is denied or invalidated by the victim—or by close or important others, such as family, friends, or helping professionals—then the person may not be able to heal completely from the adverse effects of the trauma. If the trauma continues, with still no validation and support in expressing its associated pain, it may develop into post-traumatic stress disorder (PTSD), which Rowan & Foy (1993) and others believe is a core disorder among unrecovered survivors of trauma.

To heal from trauma, the experiencer has to be able to grieve the associated pain. To grieve, the person must remember the trauma well enough to *name it accurately* (for example, "I was mugged or beaten up on the street last night.") Thus, remembering is a key to resolving the effects of the trauma (Whitfield 1995, 2010; Herman 1992). But remembering and grieving a past trauma may be difficult, since there are often roadblocks from others.

In the first Felitti et al article, ACEs, or childhood traumas, are shown to be the basis of these original 9,508 people's impairment, high-risk behaviors, disorders and disease, and early death. Called the ACE Study, it is a major epidemiological investigation on over 17,000 people of the effect of traumatic experiences during the first eighteen years of life on medical and psychiatric disease, sexual behavior, healthcare costs, and life expectancy.

From observing trauma survivors clinically, I and others have noticed and reported that they tend to have a variety of disorders or diseases at a prevalence that is higher than the general population (Whitfield 1997, 2003, 04, 10). These disorders and conditions read almost like the DSM-IV, and include: addictions (alcoholism, other chemical dependence, eating disorders, relationship and sexual addictions), dissociative disorders, including dissociative identity disorder (formerly MPD), depression and suicide attempts, anxiety disorders, borderline personality disorder, somatization disorder, psychosis, PTSD, self-harming behaviors, violent behaviors, prostitution, and pedophilia. Thus, in addition to being frequent among general medical populations, trauma survivors are often found in psychiatric and psychological outpatient clinics and practices, as well as inpatient psychiatric settings in a high frequency, some of which has been reported to range from 50 to 70% of the patients in these settings (Whitfield 1997 a & b, 2003, 04). The ACE Study and others like it provide more of both direct and circumstantial evidence to me that a substantial portion of medical and psychological illness is in large part trauma-based.

In all our history, ours is the first generation to recognize the ravages of child abuse and neglect and begin to do something about it. We are also the first generation to begin to heal ourselves physically and psychologically from the harmful effects of childhood trauma. Through trial and error and research, publication and then wider dissemination to the public, we can constructively apply our new knowledge and skill to our children. Some have suggested that if we would raise one generation of healthy children we could eradicate violence and many other problems of our world.

Carole's story not only illustrates all of the above. Her and Alex's documentary is a good start for all of us to begin to understand how to raise a generation of healthy children. It is the beginning of our own healing so we may begin to help our loved ones to grow and heal. We heal ourselves first so others can learn by example.

Charles L. Whitfield, M.D.

Atlanta, Georgia
January 2011

INTRODUCTION

I started writing this book for myself. I needed to put it down on paper so I could stop going over and over Carole's story in my mind and my heart. Her untimely death at the age of 34 tore her so quickly away from me in a way that no mother ever wants to think about. I became so obsessed with this story that I needed to park it safely on paper so perhaps I could stop going over and over it. I had hoped that this writing could help me find meaning in all the grieving I must do for the loss of Carole.

I am not her biological mother. What follows covers less than three years of our knowing each other, but in that short time she became my 'Soul daughter.' And in that short time I watched Carole's healing journey from one of the darkest of human conditions--in her own words, "a victim of very severe child sexual abuse."

I know Carole's Soul healed. I witnessed it. Her Soul, helped by her mind-- remembered and embraced all that was lost from the trauma of her childhood wounding. I am writing her story exactly as she told it to me and then the way I lived it with her.

According to Carole, her actively drinking alcoholic father raped and sodomized her from when she was an infant and throughout her childhood. Perhaps even worse, her mother never protected her even though Carole reached out in a variety of ways. She told me more than once that she would go to her mother and try to stay close to her and her mother would tell her she had to go up to the attic and play. Shortly after she went to the attic her father would come and abuse her. So just as large and looming as the sexual abuse, she needed to heal from the neglect of what we call a 'co-abuser.' (Someone who knows about the abuse, or doesn't *consciously* know, and does not help the victim.)

According to Drs. Davies and Frawley in their book *Treating the Adult Survivor of Childhood Sexual Abuse* --(Jody Messler Davies, Ph.D., Mary Gail Frawley, Ph.D., Basic Books, Harper Collins Publishers, 1994) all sexual abuse is severe. (If you have been sexually abused, please don't minimize your experience by comparing it to Carole's.) Anything of a sexual nature harms the victim's psychological and physical integrity creating rage and pain, but in silence. The offender forces the innocent child victim into silence and secrecy. Any form of child abuse, including physical, mental and emotional, or sexual abuse hurts the child and usually interrupts its healthy psychological growth and development. Psychiatrist Leonard Shengold called this child abuse "Soul Murder."

In spite of her painful past, I watched Carole transcend the pain and scars of the abuse and transform to the lightest form a human being can become-- she became a vehicle for wisdom and even a voice for Spirit in her work as a documentary film maker. This story is about Carole's healing-- and it is also about four people and how we deeply touched each other's lives.

And now, as this story is completing itself, I can see a treasure map emerging. So I feel compelled to share this. As Carole learned in her short experience on Earth, this treasure map may bring us to the greatest treasure of all-- to our Self, our Child Within -- to our Soul-- or whatever we choose to call that quietly knowable part of us that is connected to Spirit and ultimately to our God Source. Carole's journey will courageously lead the way. Her story is a beacon for all of us to awaken and reconnect with our wholeness. I am confident that whoever needs to read this story will find it.

In the first few chapters, as Carole speaks of the darkness of her childhood, the beginning of her catharsis and healing is also revealed. And then, I as the story teller am able to write:

I could feel a difference in the way it felt to be with Carole. We weren't so heavy in our conversations. We weren't talking about the darkness as much anymore... Carole and I discovered each other again as spiritual human beings. Our conversations turned more toward the Light-- toward the goodness of man. Something had shifted... We changed our outlook from the darkness to the Light.

And then I noticed:

...this new sense of something ephemeral coming from Carole. Sometimes a vague light seemed to emanate from her face.... Even when she left the room-- I could still feel her presence. It was becoming stronger. As she freed herself from the bondage of her past -- her real self started coming out and as it did she almost began to glow because the light was radiating from within her-- not from an outside source. As the years went by, looking back on all this now, it was as though it was easier to see Carole as an angel or "Tinkerbell" type fairy that had come down into a human form. She still fought all the same human mind tricks as the rest of us, but as she uncovered each new answer to make life easier, she embraced it with joy and compassion for herself and for all of us.

I completed this story and now write the introduction for a reading audience that I didn't expect when I started. But through my grieving I have come to understand that Carole's life was not just a story for me or the other people who knew and loved her. It is a story for anyone who has been touched by childhood trauma, abuse, or neglect -- for those who have suffered and dreamed of climbing out-- of disconnecting from the darkness holding them captive and of ascending to the heights of humankind-- Carole's story will show you the way.

Carole and I in the video editing suite

CHAPTER 1

CHARLIE AND I

There's a saying, *"If you want to make God laugh-- tell God your plans!"*

In 1993, we were living in Baltimore. We never thought about moving to Atlanta, where most of this story takes place. I had set my priorities and my priorities dealt with living near my adult children who lived in Florida and being in the warm sunshine. Charlie and I were going to be married the following year and he knew I was aiming for a move to Florida after we married. Little did I know we would be moving to Atlanta and that we would become great friends there with a couple that were young enough to be our children. What did we have in common? Nothing until one day in Baltimore in 1993...

Charlie was watching Donahue. He called me in to the room.

"Watch this! I can't believe what these people are saying!"

"What are they saying?" I asked.

"They're invalidating all the adults that remember abuse in their childhood... This is not good... And they're saying that if you forgot the abuse and then remember it as an adult, that your therapist planted memories that aren't real."

I saw how upset he was. Of course, if anyone would get upset it would be him because he wrote one of the first books for adults that were abused as children. It's called *Healing the Child Within* and it is still selling widely today and that includes 11 other languages all over the world. Charlie had written three more books after that on helping people to continue their healing process (as of 2011 he has 12 books on recovering from repeated trauma). And, besides his own private practice where he does individual and group therapy for adult survivors of childhood trauma, he also travels widely doing one and two day workshops to the general public on healing from childhood trauma and lectures on trauma psychology at professional conferences.

I was watching Charlie watching people on the television who were putting down everyone who was trying to heal from child abuse.

"These people on this panel have all been accused of molesting their children and they are trying to discredit their adult children. They are all saying they have been falsely accused. They can't *all* be falsely accused! My goodness, they have even formed an organization that's picking up great numbers-- so they claim. And I don't think they are screening anyone they take in."

I could see that Charlie was becoming more upset and at the same time interested in their behavior especially the blatant denial. Over time, he continued to follow this group as did his colleagues, and a few of them openly talked about it. Most were quiet though... hoping it would go away. About a year after Donahue, after Charlie did more research, he began writing a book called *Memory and Abuse* which dealt with the whole "false memory" claim that turned into mostly a dispute and at times a debate. It was one of the first comprehensive books that explained clinically how we could forget something as traumatic as child sexual abuse, and then how the memories could resurface as adults when something triggered them. And he explained other symptoms that went along with child sexual abuse that clinically were the same as what soldiers of war experienced. He described Post-traumatic Stress Disorder and traumatic amnesia. He asked,

"If Viet Nam vets forget- why can't children who have been traumatically hurt by having a sexual act forced on them, forget too?"

Charlie's stand on child abuse was one of the first big reasons why I had fallen in love with him. I had been physically and emotionally abused as a child and even though I sought therapy many times, no one ever wanted to seriously go into my child abuse, at least not the way Charlie did in his writings and teachings. He spelled out what child abuse is and then he spelled out how the aftereffects linger and affect our adult life. He explains how we can help ourselves heal. He "demystified" the healing process. Instead of having an analyst who kept everything to himself about what I was telling him, Charlie explained clearly in his books what we needed to do and how to do it to heal.

I'll never forget the first time we met. It was the last day of a conference on Consciousness Research at Georgetown University in Washington, DC. I was asking a question to the panel that had two of my colleagues on it and Charles Whitfield was in the audience. He introduced himself when the conference ended. Over the five years it took for us to meet again, I forgot what he looked like, but I did remember meeting him and I remembered thinking that he had nice energy.

After that first meeting in Washington in 1985, I went back to the University of Connecticut and continued working in research on near-death experiences and death and dying in general. And I continued healing from my divorce. I had been married for 23 years to my childhood sweetheart. We had three children who were almost grown. My near-death experience had catapulted me into new areas of growth that my 'stereotypical 50's marriage' couldn't contain.

Charlie called me occasionally and asked me research questions after we met. This went on for five years. I assumed he was just another kind doctor asking me research questions. I sent him research articles on what we had discussed usually with a brief note saying "Dear Dr. Whitfield, thank you for contacting our office and here is a journal article I know will be of interest to you. Please feel free to call on me anytime. Sincerely..."

I do remember in 1987 Charlie sent me a copy of his first book, *Healing The Child Within*. I didn't read it at that time - I just put it on the shelf with many other unread books. Many authors sent me their new books in hopes we would review them for our publication - the *Journal of Near-death Studies.*

In 1988 I was in Washington speaking on the near-death experience and a dear friend of mine, Kay Allison from Charlottesville, Virginia came in to hear my talk. She has a 'New Age' and recovery oriented bookstore and knows many in the field of personal growth and consciousness research. We were having dinner together and she asked, "Did you know that Charlie Whitfield is really sick and in ICU?" I said, "No" but we stopped and prayed together for him in the middle of this loud busy restaurant.

A LITTLE BACKGROUND

My first book *Full Circle* came out in April, 1990. To introduce it, I was to be interviewed on Larry King Live. On the Friday night before Larry King, as usual I lit my Sabbath candles because I am Jewish. I was living in a 650 square foot flat that was 80 years old in Newington, Connecticut with my two sons who were 18 and 22. Usually they both stood beside me while I lit the candles but this particular Friday evening they weren't home. I was standing alone after I said my prayers and I remember looking through the two flames and for the first time realizing that this was actually a direct line to God. I had always said prayers asking for my children and my family to be healthy and safe and that was it. This time I looked at the two sacred candles burning and thought – 'if I speak -- this will go directly to God.' That was how it felt to me. I knew it in my heart.

Writing *Full Circle* had really opened my heart again-- just as it was opened by my near-death experience (NDE). It is the story of my life, my NDE and my aftereffects that are universal to most near-death experiencers. I went from being an atheist to experiencing God in a fraction of a second in Earth time. I also had what we call a "life review" where my whole life flashed in front of me. God was holding me, and together we re-experienced my life. I not only experienced it from my perspective, but also from God's. God let me see through God's eyes and God's heart. I learned about all my relationships and what had been missing. I learned about my parents' wounding from their childhood and how that translated into the child abuse and neglect my brother and I received. I saw that we were all trapped by our past and our parents' pasts. And I experienced with God that we are really all One. Being separate is an illusion. We are all God's children and what connects us and makes us One is the Energy of God's love that we have in our hearts and we extend to each other.

This may *sound* wonderful and divine, but it's not an easy thing to know when we return to this life with all the old patterns that we and our loved ones have already made. Experiencing that we are 'all One' makes sense when we are in that other place called 'eternity.' But being back here after a childhood filled with abuse doesn't give us the protection that we need first before we can be 'One' with our loved ones. Adults like me, that were wounded by childhood abuse have usually not learned to have healthy boundaries. Here, in this reality, we need healthy boundaries first before we can become 'One' with everybody. Writing *Full Circle* had opened me again to the Oneness and to the old wounds centered around the conflict between what I learned in my NDE and what I then had to deal with because my loved ones hadn't wanted me to change.

Since my divorce I had been involved in a few relationships that turned abusive, so I stopped dating, focused on writing *Full Circle* and went back into therapy. I took a year and a half to write my book and work on boundaries and healing. Now the book was done and I had completed this 'round' of therapy.

So I looked between these two flames and I said, "Okay, God, this is it. I'm ready. Please send me..." My mind went blank and then I said, "Send me someone who is intelligent... Dear God, send me someone who is as intelligent as I am and someone who is gentle and kind." Then I took a really deep breath and said, "Send me someone I deserve." That was really scary to say - "someone I deserve." Who knows how much shadow I have left? I was scared but I had faith that I was ready for someone I deserved. Whatever that meant! (What I didn't find out until much later was that Charlie Whitfield was praying the same week for a 'healthy long-term relationship.')

Monday afternoon I flew from Hartford, Connecticut to Washington, DC. That evening on Larry King Live, Larry's wife was working in the control room, and I could hear her voice on my ear plug. She and Larry were talking back and forth when we were off camera and they were speaking with great affection. They had only known each other four months and had just gotten married. It was a whirlwind romance and they sounded so loving toward each other. I was lonely. I remember telling both of them how lucky they were.

While I was on Larry King Live, Charlie was coming home from his office and flipped on the TV and there I was - on his TV set. He said to himself, 'Barbara Harris, Barbara Harris' and he realized that he was going up to Hartford the *next* weekend to speak at an ACoA (Adult Children of Alcoholics) conference. He thought, 'I'm going to give her a call and ask her for dinner.'

Charlie called me Wednesday evening saying he had seen me on Larry King Live and would be up in my area the next weekend. Here I was praying the Friday night before. And I thought, 'Can It work this fast?'

I had a cancer patient I was seeing every evening that week for energy work (or healings) after her chemotherapy, so I told him I couldn't meet him for dinner but asked him if we could have lunch the next day. He agreed to that. Then I called my friend, Kay Allison in Charlottesville and asked her if Charlie was married. She told me he wasn't and she said she really liked him and his work. Friday morning my patient called to tell me that her chemotherapy treatment had been canceled for that day. I thought, 'well this is an interesting coincidence.' I then called Charlie in Baltimore to let him know I could meet him for dinner but he had already left for Hartford.

NEAR-DEATH RESEARCH ON CHILDHOOD ABUSE/NEGLECT/TRAUMA

Let me back up again. As part of my research on the near-death experience, we had just tied in a history of childhood abuse/neglect/trauma with people who had the ability to transcend into spiritual experiences. We showed statistically that those of us who were wounded as children learn to dissociate (as a means to protect ourselves, we 'leave' the scene) and in that process we learn to become absorbed in alternate realities. So we also are more likely to have spiritual experiences. (Not just near-death but triggered by other events, too, as shown in my second book *Spiritual Awakenings*, Health Communications, Inc.1995).

People who have not been abused or neglected as children also have spiritual experiences. But our research showed a statistically significant higher number of people who were abused having them. And we have also shown that our research population is comprised of psychologically healthy people. In the psychology/psychiatry community, this is a rather shocking and 'innovative' new approach to dissociation - reframing it in a healthy way (if the dissociation doesn't take over our lives it becomes a useful skill - even an ability). This is not shocking to the Adult Children of Alcoholics (ACoA) and recovery community - especially for those who have been abused and are now healing from their abuse. They tell us that their ability (or defense mechanism) to dissociate saved their lives.

Back in 1990 when we first showed the childhood abuse data as relevant, I wanted my colleagues to continue exploring this avenue with me but they weren't interested. Now I was going to meet Charles Whitfield, a pioneer in this recent field of childhood trauma, and I figured that before I did I would take a look at the book he had written so I would know exactly what his work was about. When I opened *Healing the Child Within* it blew me away. Everything I wanted to know - he had already written. What my colleagues had called the 'core' and 'core experience' (my NDE was a core experience) Charlie called the 'Child Within'. (This is what my second book *Spiritual Awakenings* is also about. It is a blend of the research on the aftereffects of spiritual experiences and his writing about how to heal and be who we really are - who we were in our 'core' experiences)

ACOA CONFERENCE

I hadn't been able to reach Charlie so I arrived at the hotel Friday evening unannounced. I went to the desk and asked where I could find Charlie Whitfield and was given directions to the ballroom. I walked in and there were 800 people sitting and waiting for the conference to begin. There I was at my first ACoA conference. I was so excited to talk to Charlie about his book and tell him about our latest research.

Someone asked me where my nametag was and I told her that Dr. Whitfield had invited me to attend his talk. I was shown to the 5th row, where I sat for over an hour as the introductions were made by the people who had organized the conference. There were seven or more men sitting on the podium and I kept wondering which one of them was Charlie. I couldn't remember what he looked like. Most of the men were older, stodgy and had big bellies. Finally, they introduced Dr. Charles Whitfield and his talk that was going to be on 'Feelings and Emotion.' He had been meditating in his room and so he walked in from a side door. The first thing that struck me was he was in great shape and he had to be a runner.

He talked for an hour and a half about feelings. I just sat there in astonishment. When he finished people lined up halfway around the huge room for him to sign his books that they brought. Right in the middle of signing a book, he paused, put his glasses on and looked over in my direction. I was the only one still sitting in the seats. He put down his pen, said excuse me to the person waiting, got up and walked over to me. He took my hand and said, 'I'm so glad that you could come.'

As soon as Charlie took my hand-- I knew that this man was going to greatly influence my life. I knew that right away. We ended up having dinner in a beautiful restaurant in the hotel.

Charlie told me he remembered I had worn all red when we met five years earlier. We ran out of things to say at 1:30 in the morning and I agreed to return the next day for lunch and then I offered to take him to the airport after that.

Charlie called me at 8 a.m. and asked me to come for breakfast. He said he hadn't been able to sleep all night. I hadn't slept either. I was back at the hotel at 9 o'clock. I wore all red.

I thought about him the next week and wished he would call me. Finally, Thursday evening I got up the courage to call him. His answering machine picked up and I started to leave a rather dumb message and in the middle I said, "Charlie, I'm going to cut this babble and say what's really on my mind. I really enjoyed being with you and I'd like to see you again."

He didn't return my call on Friday or Saturday. By Sunday I felt I had probably made a fool of myself and then-- he called late Sunday evening. He had been in California all week and knew when he came home he was going to call me. And there I was on his machine - saying what he was going to say to me. We made arrangements to meet the next weekend in Pennsylvania where I could attend two of his workshops 'Healing the Child Within" on Saturday and one on natural spirituality on Sunday.

The next year was a whirlwind romance; either he was flying to Connecticut or I was driving down to Baltimore. We were together more than we were apart and at the end of that year we moved in together in Baltimore.

That first year that we lived together, Charlie wrote *Boundaries and Relationships* and I wrote *Spiritual Awakenings.* We helped each other through both books. Our writing and our teaching continues to be a shared process. Together, one and one doesn't equal two anymore. The synergy between us is better than anything I could have ever dreamed of or asked for. God really did send me someone I deserved!

We lived together for three years and then we married.

Charlie and I believe that we are all 'spiritual beings' trying to have a human experience. We were spirit before we inhabited these bodies and we will be spirit again after we leave. While we are here we want to contribute as much as we can to this wonderful home we call 'Earth.' The writing that we do - we share with everyone. But we start off by sharing it with each other and then it becomes our 'work'. He gives me ideas and I give him more, too. We ask each other questions and that spurs us on to write more. We taught together and had our own individual classes at Rutgers University's Institute of Alcohol and Drug Studies.

I believe that the time has come on this planet for couples like us to find each other and get together not only for us personally, but to help work with and heal the collective community. As you will soon read, Carole and Alex believed and lived this way too.

MEMORY AND ABUSE

Every time Charlie or I start writing a new book, we talk about our hopes for the people who will read it. We get mail from our readers and we enjoy hearing how our writing has helped them. But *Memory and Abuse* felt different. When Charlie started writing it we talked more about the concerns we had for our selves. This wasn't another self-help book like we were both used to writing. This book was clearly entering a dispute that was becoming more and more heated as the "falsies" --people accused of molesting their children, with their enablers and attorneys-- made untrue claims and disseminated disinformation through the media and threatened therapists and survivors through intimidation and law suits. We talked about the possibility of us being sued. We knew the possibility could be a probability and I distinctly remember saying, "Go for it. We've always stood up for what we believed when we were alone. Now we have each other and they can't take that away. You've got to say what you know and I can't think of anyone more qualified than you." And I remember thinking that no one else seemed to have the courage at this point in the dispute because no one else was writing a book to clarify this important issue. The day the book was finished Charlie wrote the dedication. It was unlike any dedication we had written before. The last line says it all:

I DEDICATE THIS BOOK TO ALL SURVIVORS OF ABUSE

AND TO THOSE WHO CARE FOR THEM.

I WISH THERE WAS A WAY TO MAKE ALL THIS EASIER.

Meanwhile, as much as we tried, nothing would work out in the way of finding a house in Florida. We looked for almost two years, finally settling on a plan for a house that we liked but then we couldn't find land. When we finally did, the land was misrepresented by the owner and the survey was discouraging.

We were invited to Atlanta for Thanksgiving by Charlie's brother, Dick. A close friend of his is a real estate agent in Atlanta and the day after Thanksgiving we went house hunting with her. The morning of the second day, we found the house we are living in now. When we drove into the carport I fell in love. When we walked in -- I knew this was it. Two years and we couldn't make Florida work. Two days in Atlanta and we were in love with a great house five minutes from Charlie's brother. And 10 minutes from the Centers for Disease Control and Prevention (CDCP).

However, when we moved to Atlanta, we had made no contacts yet. We moved on pure faith after his contract in Baltimore was over.

ONE VOICE: THE AMERICAN COALITION FOR ABUSE AWARENESS

Before we moved to Atlanta, we spent a weekend in Washington DC at a board meeting for an organization called *One Voice: The American Coalition For Abuse Awareness*. Charlie is a member and so are several attorneys. At the beginning of the meeting he and everyone else shared their reasons for being involved in this organization that tells the truth and corrects the disinformation coming from the organization of accused child molesters.

I was grateful this group had invited us in because things were feeling pretty lonely for us. We were being sued as we had feared by the husband and wife who were the founders of the organization for accused child molesters. They sounded like they were trying to silence Charlie by threatening our financial security. Neither Charlie nor I had ever been through a law suit before and at times we became overwhelmed. This was clearly a "slapp" suit which means a trivial suit to intimidate and try to silence. As time went by and we worked with our lawyers -- it became clear to both of us that this law suit was propelling Charlie to further define the traits of a molester and "co-abuser" (or enabler) so they could be more easily recognized. This not only helped our attorneys but then helped the profession more easily recognize and understand the way child molesters react from a psychodynamic perspective.

Moving and being sued at the same time was playing havoc on our stress levels. Being with the people on the board of *One*

Voice made us both feel better even if it was just for a weekend. Then they were only a phone call away and we heard from them through e-mail all the time because they became a clearing house for all the information as it came in.

CHAPTER 2

ALEX AND CAROLE

Meanwhile, Alex and Carole had met and married one month before we did. They had moved to Atlanta shortly before us and because of a huge debate with her parents about her recovered memories of sexual abuse in her childhood-- had contacted *One Voice.* Alex and Carole are documentary film makers and they wanted to do research for a documentary they were planning on doing to expose this organization that was founded and run by the couple who were suing us.

Eileen King, the executive director of *One Voice,*(Now *Justice for Children*) realized we were in the same town and called us, saying, "If you're interested in meeting this couple, I can give you their phone number." She had asked them for permission-- telling them who we were and not wanting to give out our phone number.

SUN MOON STARS

I called Alex and Carole the next day and we made plans to meet on the weekend. Atlanta is a huge city, but they lived only ten minutes from us. I spent the rest of the week working in our new- old kitchen. The house was almost thirty years old and I still couldn't understand why-- even in the early 70's anyone would pick revolutionary soldiers with muskets for some of the tiles on our kitchen back splash. I had some wrapping paper with suns, moons and stars on it and started cutting them to the size of the squares of the picture tiles. I thought, "I have nothing to lose by trying." I rubbed decoupage paste on one tile and stuck up a star. When it dried I sprayed it with clear polyurethane paint. I did a few more and waited to see if they would fall off. (That was 14 years ago and they're still stuck tight.)   I spent Wednesday, Thursday and Friday gluing suns, moons and stars to my kitchen tile. In between -- just to get out because I thought I was going to go blind or my fingers were going to be permanently stuck together from all the glue-- I went to several stores and found pretty decorations of suns, moons and stars from picture frames to sand sculptures and even some beautiful carved suns with big smiley faces. The kitchen became celestial and I figured this was totally original. (This was before the celestial craze happened.)

That weekend, as we walked into Carole and Alex's house for the first time, I couldn't believe my eyes; the entire place was decorated with suns, moons and stars. And the name of their television production company was "Celestial Stars." I told them about what I had just finished in our kitchen and they smiled. But a week later when they walked into our kitchen-- their response was immediate and much bigger. We giggled and glowed in the coincidence and Charlie and I told them about *synchonicities*-- meaningful coincidences that happen much more often than is normal and present some kind of a theme that leaves us feeling that something greater than us is influencing what is happening. And, synchronicities transcend the explanation of cause and effect in our lives. (The four of us started talking at once--something that we did often because of the excitement we shared.) This was a spiritual explanation for meaningful coincidences and we agreed it was true.

We had so much in common with this young couple that the visits became biweekly and sometimes more often. It didn't matter that we were in our late 50's and they were just turning 30. We shared all our stories-- our individual histories and our romantic stories.

As we got to know them better, they told us how they met. They knew almost immediately that they were Soul mates. Alex went first. "We met on St. Patrick's Day, 1992 in a New York subway station, both of us waiting to return home to Hoboken. I remember the night clearly. The moment I saw her I knew I had to meet this girl. I asked her if this was the right train to Hoboken, explaining that I had just moved and wasn't sure... Well I kind of knew but she assured me I was going the right way. I introduced myself and she gave me her card which had her picture on it. I thought she was the most beautiful woman I had ever met in my life. I insisted on walking her home and she politely shook my hand goodnight. I was on cloud nine. The next day I quickly got out her card and found out I wasn't dreaming. I got up the nerve to call her and she remembered me but declined my offer to dinner saying that she just broke up with someone and wasn't interested. I hung up dejected but after my friend convinced me not to give up I went out in a terrible snow storm, hand-picked the biggest bouquet of flowers and tried again. This time she said 'yes.'

"Literally from our first date we fell madly in love-- each asking the other 'where have you been?' Once together, it was years before we even spent just one day apart. Carole is my Soul mate."

Carole sat in silence for a moment obviously drinking in what Alex had just said. And then she told us her recollections, "From the moment I got into his cool little car-- I know I was struck by cupid's arrow. It's a feeling I will never forget-- sitting across from Alex at dinner, knowing him without ever having known him. I thought-- someone is playing a trick on me. Everything he had to say and feel, I did too. He understood me and I really thought at that point, that no one would ever understand me or share the same views in life.

Carole, smiling into Alex's eyes, said, "The angels were looking down and smiling the day you *finally* found me waiting for the train. It was a split second in eternity that was all ours. Time stopped. From that day on, you and I have been on a very exciting path, growing together and learning the ways of the world."

They were married just three weeks before us. When we became friends-- we were all still newlyweds.

Carole said Charlie was her hero because she was an ACoA and an abuse survivor, too. (She told me later that the first time we agreed to come over she couldn't believe *he* was actually coming to *her* house. She said his writings had validated her childhood.) And she believed that we were being sued by the same couple who had mentored *her parents* in starting a chapter of that same group in their home town.

When we first met, Carole was tortured about all this. She was thin, almost anorexic and she smoked heavily and paced all the time. She told me that the acne she was suffering with had only begun a few years ago with the big upheaval with her parents. Before that her skin was beautiful. Carole also suffered from migraine headaches which subsided shortly after we met. Both she and Alex were heavy smokers. We talked with them often about their stress level and how to help themselves. They wanted to work their stress out by doing a documentary exposing these accused child molesters that were not only generating disinformation to the media but were also organizing legally to sue everyone they could who disagreed with them publicly -- and claiming that they, the accused child molesters, were the victims. Carole said they were bullying the media into believing their denial-- just like they bullied their victims and anyone who criticized them or in any way tried to expose their abusive criminal treatment of children.

We sat for hours in Carole and Alex's living room and talked about all this. They sat on one sofa and we on the other, facing each other. Carole, with her long brown hair and deep set hazel eyes would go deeper and deeper into all the implications of this vast and painful subject that most people won't talk about.

ABUSERS AND CO-ABUSERS

"I wonder how many of those parents who have been accused are alcoholics?" She asked, "I wonder how many of them have blackouts and just don't remember what they did? My father is a heavy drinker. My mother's father was an alcoholic. She just fell in the same pattern enabling the alcoholism and ultimately enabling the abuse. I often wonder if my mother was abused herself. I read that abuse victims often will partner with abusers and later repeat the abuse. My sister and I are pretty sure he is an alcoholic. How can any of them be so sure they didn't sexually or physically harm their kids when they can't even remember *anything* after they drink. I know the man who is suing you is an admitted alcoholic. How can he be so sure he is innocent? Maybe it's he who has the 'false memory.' When my father confessed he said even though he had no memory of abusing us, he realized he could have had blackouts while drunk.

"Charlie, my mother is a typical 'co-abuser.' She *let* my father abuse us. And then she covered it up-- even *after* he confessed. I've talked with other abuse survivors about the 'other' parent-- the one who didn't do it-- and I believe my mother is just as guilty. And she is so worried about what others will think. That's all she ever worries about. She pretends it didn't happen -- and to do that she shut down all her feelings. Have you ever thought of looking at this?"

Charlie nodded, "Perhaps the best kind of study to answer your questions would be a clinical research one where over time clinicians get to know co-abusers and their experience intimately and then report their findings. My clinical experience is that some co-abusers actually did not know that their children were being sexually abused. They were out of the house when it happened. So I think some co-abusers or co-offenders care as much about their child and knowing what happened to try to prevent more in the future that they will take an open look without reflexively defending the abuser and invalidating the experience of the abuse survivor."

"JUNK DEALERS-UNDER THE VEIL OF SCIENCE"

We knew the same names in this long list of characters. Before we met Alex and Carole we also suspected many of them. We along with Carole and Alex, had seen through the pretense and knew these people were making a lot of money testifying as "expert witnesses" in pumped up law suits aimed at destroying the lives of psychotherapists who had treated sexual abuse survivors. The parents (who were accused by their own children) made themselves out to be the victims of "false memory syndrome." This is a name that was made up by the organization and in fact had never been and to this day has still not been documented in any peer-reviewed scientific journal.

When they showed us their proposal for the documentary [1] they were calling *Junk Dealers: Under the Veil of Science*-- the first two pages shocked me because they were so visually powerful.

---

[1] Alex and Carole had already received awards for their work as documentary film makers. I was beginning to understand why.

The first page showed a little girl with a big black eye. In a child's printing the caption said, "I've got my mothers eyes." The next page showed a very young pregnant girl in profile. Her huge belly was protruding from her open robe as she looked down at it. The caption said, "We both have the same Father."

Carole read us her synopsis of the proposal: "Our government reports that sexual criminals are the fastest growing segment of our overcrowded prison population, yet a vast majority of child sexual abuse goes unreported and unprosecuted. These unprotected children suffer lifelong damage and often become re-victimized or go on to become abusers themselves thus compounding a problem already cycling out of control.

"'Junk Dealers' is an expose on the purveyors of junk science and the tactics they use to silence victims of abuse. Junk science has infiltrated our courtrooms and manipulated our media with disinformation. The damage is severe and far reaching, directly impacting our children and how we are able-- or not able-- to protect them.

"These unproved theories supported by a small minority of scientists are used as a smoke and mirrors defense, letting child molesters go free. In a crime where any direct evidence is often hard to come by, the junk scientists are promoting their theories using highly paid expert witnesses and consultants, convincing judges and juries that children and adults who say they were sexually abused cannot and should not be believed.

"This organization that supports and promotes these 'scientific' expert witnesses is comprised of people that have been accused of sexually molesting children. Their only real defense is their denial. They have elaborately constructed this organization to promote 'junk science,' to influence the media and to sue-- not only their accusers-- but also the health care professionals that support the victim's healing.

"It is estimated that at least one in four women and one in five men have been sexually abused by the time they reach the age of eighteen. The Center for Disease Control and Prevention has done the largest known study to date evidencing a causal relationship between a history of childhood sexual abuse and its aftereffects-- including alcoholism and drug dependence, criminal behavior, physical illnesses, eating disorders, prostitution, rape and mental illness.

"These fabricated pseudoscientific terms such as "false memory syndrome (fms)," "parental alienation syndrome (pas)," and "recovered memory therapy (rmt)," have been peddled along with cries of a 'witch hunt' and an 'epidemic of false accusations.' Yet, The American Prosecutors Society and The National Center for the Defense of Child Abuse also believes that the historically small percentage of false allegations in child sexual abuse cases remains constant today.

"The junk scientists create controversial claims and then demand others to prove them wrong instead of being able to prove they are right. We intend to expose this convoluted process they have invented and set the record straight."

We sat in silence for several minutes trying to absorb all she had said in only one page.

I thought about how Carole and Alex were wise beyond their years. I felt we were drawn to them in a way that Souls find each other and call the instant familiarity-- 'Soul family.' And, partly we were drawn to each other because --on a more practical note-- we were being sued by the same people Carole and Alex were drawn to expose.

Alex broke the silence saying, "when you strip away all their hype-- they are an organization of accused child molesters who are denying their guilt and blaming anyone else they can. It's a long hard explanation but who do we want to believe -- accused child molesters or a scientific body of literature that is now bursting with proof that we forget traumas in our childhood that are too horrific to deal with and then -- as adults-- something triggers us into remembering. And it's usually not a therapist. It could be anything that brings back our memories through flashbacks, a simple smell, a sound..."

These discussions would create a tension in Carole and in me. Every time we talked about the actual aftereffects: the flashbacks, the body memories, a sound or smell that provokes a sense of fear, anything like that and both she and I would cringe. My abuse had been physical, not as secret, covered up and denied as sexual abuse, but it had been often and severe and was buried deeply in my body like Carole's was buried deeply in hers. We thereby shared and felt a commonality that was understood in eye contact or suddenly needing to get up and walk for a few minutes or get some air outside. Even though I had had years of psychotherapy and body work, I was still sensitive to triggers that reminded my mind and my body of my childhood pain.

Carole had been in therapy before and as all this started coming up for her again, I could see her becoming more sad and agitated. I asked her if she would go back into therapy because I was worried about her. Looking back on all this now, I realize that Carole trusted me so much that she would agree to most anything I suggested. So she went back into therapy and she started her psychological and emotional healing in deeper ways. That took pressure off of Charlie and me. We didn't have to think as therapists with Carole. We could watch her move through her pain and just be with her as friends.

WHO IS RESPONSIBLE?

The night Carole pulled out a letter from her father was probably the hardest one for me. He had written it in 1992 by hand and had written the identical letter to Carole's sister. It read:

Dear Carole,

I want you to know how distraught and upset I have been over the Knowledge of My actions of sexual abuse in our family. I am ashamed. I am fully aware of the pain I am undergoing. Your suffering must be even worse if that is possible. I want so desperately to have you clearly hear and then accept my apology for what has happened. I am at your mercy for this and pray that your wounded heart will allow it. Please hear the intentions of my words as they are coming directly from my heart and out of my deep love for you.

I wanted to wait until I received some sort of signal from you that you were ready to see me personally before I communicated my apology and also my understanding of the causes for this and other family dynamics. That is the reason for such poor timing on my part. While I do not have all the pieces sorted out yet I have made light years of progress in my understanding of events and want to share these with you as soon as possible. The book I sent you was meant to give you a perspective of how I am changing and give you comfort in the thought of a personal discussion. I hope you can accept this gift as coming directly from my heart and out of my deep love for you too.

I have asked mom to join us in our discussions. I am proposing we come to visit with you in NY on Sat. night Dec. 12. If this isn't a good time please let me know when is. I have so much to say.

I love you,
Dad

When Carole finished reading her dad's letter, Charlie said, "While I believe his confession, only about less than 3% of child molesters confess and probably a smaller percentage actually put it in writing. This looks like strong evidence that he did abuse you and I would guess that it validates your story. Carole, I'm so sorry for your pain."

Carole sat quietly for a moment. Her face flushed and her eyes were now wet. "Thank you, Charlie. I appreciate you going over all this with me. I need it so much!"

Then Carole pulled out drawings with stick figures made by her 10 year old niece. They depicted scenes when she was with her grandfather. One shows a figure lying down. Next to him but not part of the scene, is a pair of pants with something drawn between the legs that roughly resembled a penis. She printed "After he drank he walked a little different and he looked dizzy. It scared me. I'm seeing grand pa drinking Alkhal." She called this page "Drinking at Cottage." In another picture she shows herself and grand pa on a tractor. She printed underneath, "I'm sitting on the tractor and while every once and a while grandpa would pull me up by the --drawing of pants-- and I didn't fell right. (her spelling) I also could feel his --drawing of a pair of pants with a projection-- It felt like a rock and it was a little Hard."

I sat there feeling numb as we went through more drawings. Now that we were seeing actual illustrations of what the grandchildren were reporting, with the confession note from her dad, we became more confused about Carole's own story. It seems that she had forgotten the abuse from her childhood or perhaps, she said, "It was always there in the back of my mind- but it was faded and in the shadows."

However, when her sister, who says she never forgot the abuse, told Carole about it several years ago, Carole's memories surfaced again. They confronted their father and shortly after received the letter from him. Somewhere in there though -- he wanted them to go to *his* therapist-- who he would pay for and "they could heal." Meanwhile, his wife, Carole's mother, wanted to divorce him, and moved into Carole's sister's house. Carole said, "Although I was happy for the apology, I wasn't convinced that his immediate turn around and road to recovery were as contrite as reported. My father's need to control the situation reminded me of his illness. His need to control me and my sister made us suspicious that he was just saying what we wanted to hear. Also, we were not allowed to feel the anger we felt. He wanted it all just to go away but somehow it didn't seem fair. It didn't feel just."

Carole was becoming more upset. Alex sat down on the arm of her chair and draped himself around her, cloistering her in his huge body so that she would catch her breath. I watched him wait for her to breathe and then he continued the story, "The more they pressed him to own his actions and take responsibility, the more he would back away. His words were guarded as if guided by a lawyer or therapist or both.

Meanwhile, Carole's mother was acting as a child herself. Invading the privacy of her daughters and acting as a dependent, helpless child the whole time they were both trying to put their father's actions into perspective—Carole's mother asked perpetually in different ways what would become of her.

As the sisters started sharing memories they both had, sometimes for the first time since they happened-- waves of emotion and release occurred. After awhile they started probing questions of who else knew in the family. Where was Mom when all this was going on? When they confronted her she denied any knowledge of what had happened, but both sisters looked at each other and agreed "You know Mom, you were there, we remember.

We remember you pulling him off of us to bring him back to bed after he passed out. You knew! Why didn't you do anything?"

Immediately following this confrontation Carole's mother began meeting secretly with their father. She was reconciling with him without telling Carole or her sister and then asked the girls continuous questions as to what they were going to do now. Carole and her sister didn't know what their mother was doing. They were still trying to make sense of everything--reliving each memory, confounded by the pain and the lie that they had been forced to live.

While still separated, Carole's mother went for a short visit with relatives in another town where an advisory board member of the organization for accused child molesters lived. Carole's mother visited the board member who convinced her that this was another case of 'false memory syndrome'. Carole's mother flew home and immediately moved back in with her husband. That same day he bought her an expensive luxury automobile.

Shortly after all this happened, Carole's sister's husband moved out and sued her for divorce. He got custody of their three young children and Oh! This part is so hard to get! Several times a week he had Carole's parents baby-sitting, after school and when he went out of town. That's where these drawings came from.

I asked Carole to tell us parts of this unbelievable story again because I was having trouble following it-- or maybe my confusion came from trying to *believe* it. What was confusing me the most was how our whole legal system had failed. These three young children were being delivered into the hands of a self-confessed pedophile.

Carole explained that her sister was portrayed as being incapable of caring for her children. Much that she was accused of in that respect, happened to be symptoms of having been sexually abused as a child. Carole went on to say that politics and every other aspect of their town was controlled by a "good old boy" network and the town was pretty much "bought." Legally her sister couldn't get anywhere. Carole, in an act of final desperation before she removed herself (as much as she could) from all this, made copies of her father's confession, the children's drawings and an explanation from her and sent all this material to the local newspapers. She put this heading on it: *Known Self-admitted Pedophile now has granddaughter drawing graphic pictures of their interaction-- who's Responsible?*

Her explanation reads: My sister and I were both sexually abused our entire childhood by our father. On May 17, 1995 my sister lost custody of her three children as a result of being labeled because of the abuse. The pedophile has admitted to his sexual abuse in writing, however, the court is permitting custody to her ex-husband who regularly puts the children in the care of this known abuser. I believe it is criminal neglect for a father to knowingly place his children in the hands of an admitted pedophile. Who is responsible for the welfare of these children? Is this not criminal endangerment of a child under a penal code? These drawings are recent expressions of my 10 year old niece's experiences alone with her grandfather. Does another tragedy have to happen? These children need to be protected from this vicious crime. Sole custody should be restored to my sister and appropriate action taken against this sick pedophile and negligent father. Who is responsible?

Advice: Please HELP

Carole pulled out more papers-- legal papers, her outlines of family trees and timetables to explain how all this had happened. She showed us letters about a law suit she and her sister had started. They finally had to give up the suit because the laws and decisions were already being affected by the 'falsies'(the organization of accused child molesters) efforts: court cases being lost and bills being introduced in federal and state legislatures that covertly took the justice away from victims of child abuse.

Carole went on to tell us that in February of 1994, her sister and brother-in-law, when they were still married, had changed their Last Will and Testament stating that in the event of their death, Alex and Carole would be the children's guardian and in no circumstance, would Carole's parents have any visitation with the children.

"So how," Carole asked, "could my brother-in-law now willfully hand his children over to my father and mother? And how could my mother go away and leave each child alone with him?

"We all tried to move on in our lives and deal with the tremendous strain that comes along with being sexually abused your whole childhood. What a coincidence that this is just about the same time that our parents supposedly founded the 'falsie's' chapter in my home town.

"On September 16, 1994, my sister's husband requested and was granted an Ex-Parte Hearing for Divorce and Custody in the Supreme Court of Pennsylvania. A law guardian was assigned by the judge to the children. (This lawyer was paid for by MY brother-in-law who received financial assistance from my parents!) Psychological tests for my sister and brother-in-law were also ordered and conducted by a forensic psychiatrist, an expert also hired by HIM. The children are still seeing this therapist who *consults with my parents* before the children's sessions and tells the kids at every session that they have never been abused. Talk about implanting ideas or thoughts into a child's head! This seems to me to be a major case of criminal malpractice!"

As Carole went on with her story I could see that she was becoming more and more stressed. My heart was breaking for her and at the same time I saw she wasn't breathing-- a common symptom for those of us who have suffered any kind of childhood abuse.

"Carole, Honey," I said softly, looking into her eyes. "Stop a moment and take a deep breath... This story is deeply hurting me to hear, so it must *really* be hurting you. Are you all right?"

Carole was quiet a moment and said, "Yea! It hurts. But it feels good to tell you both because I want you to know... I want you to know Charlie, how important your work is and how much you're helping me and why you are my hero."

Charlie nodded, looking sad. "Please go on with this story." he said.

She continued, "The actual Custody trial lasted for two weeks in the State Supreme Court. My sister's counseling records regarding the sexual abuse done to her by our father were dragged through court in an attempt to make my sister look unstable and label her with a disorder. Meanwhile, her husband's counseling records were never examined, or the fact that he was on anti-depressants and other pills. To make a long story short, my sister lost custody of her three children, sole custody was given to him 'in the best interest of the children' and by the recommendation of the law guardian and psychiatrist. It doesn't matter that the children all stated they preferred to live with their mother or that she was available to take care of them 24 hours a day, which she had done since they were born. When the court asked who would take care of the children while their father was working, he initially verbally promised the court he would not allow the children to be alone or unsupervised with our father.

"Since then, the children have been continually placed in the care of our father. They have told me on tape that they have to go to our father's house separately, one at a time for "alone time" with grandpa. My brother-in-law, who was always in debt the entire time he was married to my sister, now has spent $54,000 on legal fees, has a new car, a new job and a new girlfriend-- and I wonder how 'new' she is. It is uncanny how his girlfriend's daughter who is three, looks just like his daughter. We wonder -- the age and time frame of events would fit perfectly.

"Although the judge was given a copy of our father's letter admitting he is a child molester, the eldest child has drawn pictures of the abuse and her grandfather's penis, and a report was filed with Child Protective Services, nothing has been done to prevent the children from spending time unsupervised with our father!"

Carole was now so upset that her fists were clenched, but I knew nothing could stop her. She went on. "It is well documented and statistics show that child molesters do not get 'cured' by themselves. They do not just stop, they go on to continue their abuse to children over and over again. Now it's not just my sister's three children who are vulnerable to his abuse, it is the children's friends and other children on the baseball teams our father was the umpire for this summer. Children give access to more children.

"It is apparent that money buys justice and freedom in this country. My sister has no rights as far as her children are concerned and is not even allowed to legally take them to a therapist interested in HELPING the children. She is broke and just trying to survive. We feel our hands have been tied, but we will not give up the fight to free these precious three children and others from this sick, Soul-destroying sexual abuse. This is our fight to get some help, to try and make the system work and to find out who is responsible."

MEMORIES, ABUSERS AND ALCOHOLISM

Charlie and I sat in silence. We had been feeling our own frustration for so long. And now we were hearing Carole's. It didn't make us feel any better and we knew we couldn't take away her pain. I realized how much pain I was in. I felt tears dripping down my face and splashing on my shirt.... Alex sat silently on the arm of Carole's chair. He was again leaning over in a way that encircled her-- as though he was using his body to protect her. I sat and neatly organized all the papers Carole had given us-- her niece's implicating pictures of their grandfather with them plus transcripts of recent taped conversations with the children and their father Jim, Carole's father's handwritten confession, timelines and incriminating family trees she had written. I filed them away. I could not look at the papers. I would also file away the memory of her saying *rape* and *sodomy*. I could not or would not connect those words with the idea of her experiencing them as an infant and child. I defensively numbed out to the horror she could not escape.

Needless to say Alex had never been able to numb out. He was in this all the way with Carole. Alex, gifted with intelligence and eloquence, told Charlie, "I understand the importance in *real* science of being published in *peer reviewed publications*. You are objectively refuting the claims of the false memory advocates and defending the experience of survivors and their therapists by writing papers that are published in *peer reviewed journals.* Your book *Memory and Abuse* has to be the first clear and comprehensive description of memory and trauma and the way offenders are able to deny their guilt."

My heart lifted a little when I saw Carole's face light up as she said to Charlie, "Now you know why you're my hero."

Among all of her papers, Carole pulled out a recently published book review on Charlie's book *Memory and Abuse.* She placed her finger on the last paragraph of the review and read, "Because *Memory and Abuse* helps those of us who are the faces behind the statistics honor the truth of our memories, it is a valuable book. For the ammunition it provides to refute those who say we are lying, it is even more valuable. This book helps take our recovery back into our own hands, regardless of the claims of the [organization of accused parents and others.]"

Carole paused a moment and then finished, "In recovery… we learn that *no one else* any longer *determines our destiny*," Whitfield writes. "Rather, by our own motivation and by setting healthy boundaries, we create it."

One evening Alex handed me a poem he had just written. I think this poem beautifully illustrates his profound understanding and compassion:

THE CHILD WHO CRIED

THE WHOLE WORLD KNOWS THE CHILD WHO CRIED,
FROM THE SINS OF THE FATHER, WHICH WE ALL ABIDE.
CREATOR, NOW CREATURE, UNDER BLANKETS THEY HIDE
THE WHOLE WORLD PAYS WHEN THEIR SPIRIT HAS DIED.

THE WHOLE WORLD KNOWS WHERE TO FIND FEAR.
SOUL MURDER AT MIDNIGHT, THE BATTERED TEAR.
BETRAYAL, BRUTAL, FORGETTING THE PAIN.
PLEAS FOR HELP, CRY OUT IN VAIN.

THE WHOLE WORLD KNOWS WHY THE CHILD CRIED.
WE FEIGN THAT WE CARE, TO OURSELVES WE HAVE LIED.

THE WHOLE WORLD KNOWS HOW WE LIVE WITH THE RAGE.
THE CHILDREN NOT HEARD WE LOCK IN A CAGE.
ADDICTION, VIOLENCE, LIFE IN A DAZE,
BECOMING THE PARENT THAT THEIR PARENTS RAISED.

THE WHOLE WORLD SUFFERS FOR THE CHILDREN DENIED
WHETHER THE CHILD WITHIN OR THE ONE BY OUR SIDE.
REACH OUT, LISTEN, OPEN YOUR EYES
PROTECT THE CHILDREN, REJECT THE LIES.

THE WORLD KNOWS, BUT DOES NOT HEAR
THE CHILD WHO CRIES, SILENCED IN FEAR.

So we went through months with Carole and Alex, listening, shaking our heads and following our hearts by being there for these two young beautiful people. And their stories soothed our fear in this awful lawsuit that had been waged against us. Carole would look deeply into my eyes and remind me often that Charlie and my pain over the law suit was worth it. She would pump me up when my strength and hope would languish-- telling me we were spiritual warriors using truth instead of swords.

And when Carole was low she talked about her mother. She said she was more hurt by her mother than her dad. "I know my mother's father was an alcoholic and she covered for him and then she covered for my father. And you know why? She is so worried about appearances – that's why. That's all she cares about. We always had to look good when we were out in public. She always looks perfect. But she never protected us. Charlie, what's been your experience with mothers and families like mine?"

"I've seen a lot of families with addiction and co-addiction. I've also surveyed about 2000 adult children of alcoholics and other dysfunctional parents. I've found that about two thirds of these recovering ACoAs reported that their family was like yours, i.e. the 'looking good' kind. About a fourth report that their families were not 'looking good,' but to most observers when they were children, both outside and inside the family, their family appeared 'crazy' or troubled. The other five to ten percent said their family was somewhere in between. Of course, over time, some 'looking good' families transition or evolve into more overtly troubled appearing families."

Then Carole asked, "Charlie, what did you call them--I guess stereotypically-- the mothers? Do you call them 'Co-abusers?' Are all co-abusers from alcoholic families or do they only just care about what other people think, so they protect the abuser and don't protect their own kids?"

Charlie answered, "I don't know-- we need more research. Right now, I'm researching the traits of the abuser. I'm sitting in on and observing two psychotherapy groups every week for admitted and convicted pedophiles. As for co-abusers, I've researched much of the literature and have several patients, long-term, who were co-abusers. I've also observed the words and behaviors of several co-abusers who deny the abuse, and some have been members of the organized group of accused molesters that you so eloquently call 'The Falsies.'"

THE BODY KEEPS THE SCORE

When Carole held her breath while telling us something painful, I would often ask her to stop a moment and breathe deeply. She would stop and look in my eyes. It took her a few seconds to get in touch with her breath, as though she had to go deep inside and find it, and then we would breathe together. Finally, the two of us in a moment of silliness got on her computer and printed out the word *"**breathe**"* in large italicized letters. We framed it and then hung it where she would see it all the time.

On occasion I went to a doctor with her when Alex couldn't go and she needed moral support. For a woman in her early 30's, Carole had many health problems with complications much more often than the average.

Now Carole had developed cystic acne. She had perfect skin until a few years ago when all the problems with her family had erupted. We talked often with Charlie about the parallels. We discussed the ramifications of child abuse on our adult lives if the traumas weren't dealt with. He told us, "Trauma survivors seem to get chronic and acute illnesses more than people that grew up in a healthy family. Part of that is related to an unhealthy life style which may include nicotine, alcohol and other addictions-- even food and overwork. So already having post-traumatic stress disorder (PTSD) most trauma survivors accumulate even more stress. And unhealed stress -- or distress-- is a causal factor in their diseases. Stress is dis-ease – meaning 'to be without ease!'"

My respiratory therapy training and my work with sexual abuse survivors had also taught me about PTSD. I saw all of the workings in the physical body of survivors as connected to the inhibited breath cycle. I continued the discussion by adding, "The stress can be somewhat alleviated by learning to breathe into it. That's why your psychotherapist and I are telling you to breathe when you don't know you've stopped. If all of us learned better techniques of breathing, we may not need anti-anxiety medication, muscle relaxants or tranquilizers. I learned more about healthy breathing when I went to massage therapy school than when I was in training to become a respiratory therapist. All I learned there was about abnormal breathing. I learned about dis-ease in massage therapy school as we *experienced* relaxation through massage, we were also coached by our instructors to breathe. The best examples of healthy breathing that I learned came from Asian techniques like Shiatsu. So now I remember -- when I don't forget-- to breathe when I start to feel frozen or numb. When I remember to breathe in-- I can be present with what is and I can be myself, not my frightened or negative ego. And Charlie and I stress in our work that a big part of healing comes from being able to tolerate emotional pain. We stay with it. We don't allow ourselves to numb out anymore. We can help ourselves through experiencing the painful feelings by breathing and staying present and eventually the emotional pain dissipates. We move through it [metabolize it] and eventually it disappears instead of being trapped. "

"Otherwise," Charlie added. "The body keeps the score. That means-- getting in touch with and experiencing your emotional pain or eventually-- your body will express it through disease."

I added, "That's why I loved my training in massage therapy. The school took a holistic approach. My teachers understood how a history of child abuse holds and freezes the body and creates blockages in the natural flow of energy and metabolism.

"Carole, you should be going for massages and often..."

Carole understood what we were saying about the effects of child abuse. She always did. She made an appointment that week for a massage and then continued every week after.

Both Charlie and I had been writing and teaching for years and now Carole and Alex understood and embraced what we had to offer. Whenever Charlie and I went to teach at a conference or university, when we came back we told Carole and Alex about what we learned while attending some of the other lectures, and they took it all in.

CHAPTER 3

INTO THE SPOTLIGHT

Until now I had been reserved with Alex and Carole about my own research. I figured that what we had in common was child abuse and for now that was where it needed to stay. Occasionally, we forgot our common denominator and just had a nice time with them-- lunches or dinners out -- or the four of us would take turns preparing a meal. Then Carole developed eczema on the palms of her hands and the bottoms of her feet. I remembered having eczema as a child - in the creases inside my elbows and how much it hurt. My rash had been bandaged all the time so I could never scratch. Carole's hands and feet were open and looked crusted and inflamed, sometimes they bled.

Eventually I explained that in my research we had looked at the aftereffects of having a near-death experience and one of them is having the ability to transfer "healing energy" to others. I had been doing healing sessions for years and I asked Carole if we could try to do some healing work on her hands and feet. She agreed. So Carole and I got together two or three times a week and "meditated" while she placed her two hands on mine and then after ten minutes or so I would switch to holding her feet. We began each session with a prayer. The rash started to improve.

We often discussed that *one* of the causes of eczema is stress. Slowly Carole began to learn how to relax. She said that as soon as we started to pray and she felt my hands, she could feel the energy moving through her and she could let go of her stress in a way that she didn't know about before. I was encouraged with her because I know the tension we can carry from our abuse. It continues because we don't know how else to feel until we are shown experientially. Carole was catching on. And, sitting with her several times a week--praying together for her healing-- and holding her hands and feet over 15 to 20 minutes-- opened us to a deeper closeness.

Sometimes we would talk about all the coincidences-- all the synchronicities that were happening between and around us. Sometimes one of us would say something that the other was about to say. Sometimes we would be silent for a long period and then discuss the comfort of being in the silence together in a way that is hard to find words for.

WE WIN THE LAWSUIT

In the fall, Charlie and I had a couple of months of chaos in our new thirty year old home. We had contracted to have a wall between a spare bedroom and our bathroom removed and made into one large bathroom. We lived with the noise and mess for eight weeks until the work was completed. I painted our new wonderful bathroom myself. It was a labor of love. I spent days sanding doors and the woodwork. I put three coats of paint on the upper walls and ceiling. I took great pride in my work. I was up on the ladder putting the final coat of gloss on the door jams (as usual—I was covered in paint,) Charlie walked in and said, "Come down off the ladder."

"Why?" I asked. "I'm almost through here. Just a few more minutes."

"Come down off the ladder." Charlie said firmly, but I could tell there was a mischievous sound somewhere between "come down" and "the ladder."

"What?" I said as I came down, wiping the paint from my hands onto the back of my jeans.

He looked me straight in the eye and said very calmly, "We won the lawsuit!"

I threw my arms around him and was muffling my screaming in his shoulder. My body was jumping up and down and I couldn't stop shaking. I was laughing and crying at the same time. This law suit had hung over us like a terrible chronic illness for over a year and a half now and it was finally over. There was a time when I thought it would never end, and now it was finally over.

"Let's call the attorneys back. Let's call my brother. Let's call Carole and Alex!" I wanted the world to know. And "We won. We won!"

I knew we would win but I always had that feeling of dread behind the knowing. What if the judge was a pedophile or an active alcoholic? And I always worried in the back of my mind. I was never sure about trusting the "Justice System." But we won! I could believe again in justice...

As soon as I told Carole, she had to hang up and call Alex at work. They came over that evening and we celebrated.

The only thing that was hard for Carole and Alex when we got together was their smoking cigarettes. Every visit found us out on the deck-- theirs or ours-- in all kinds of weather.

I remember a Halloween party that they had. It was cold. All of their smoking friends were out in their carport standing in a circle talking and smoking. We non-smokers were in the house socializing. Carole and Alex would move back and forth but I don't remember ever meeting their smoking friends. I do remember Carole and Alex looking especially cute that evening. They wore black pants and black tops. On each of their backs was a box of cereal and sticking out of the box was a knife. They were "cereal killers."

CAMILLA SCOTT SHOW

Christmas was almost here and I received a phone call from a television producer I knew from Canada. When I worked in research at the University of Connecticut I had been involved in too many TV shows to count anymore. I was either on myself or supplied guests for many of the talk shows including Oprah, Donahue, Joan Rivers and news shows including CNN Medical News, CBS Evening News, Good Morning America, The Today Show and more. My favorites were the foreign documentaries-- France, Belgium, Germany, Italy, Canada and Japan. Other countries were more open than the U.S. and willing to explore the compilation of revelations near-death experiencers had told us about in our research. Even the United States was beginning to be interested in the phenomena called the near-death experience. And when I left the university I thought my days of doing TV work were over. But occasionally I still get a call from a producer that remembered me and wanted me to come on a show or perhaps if I couldn't -- they asked if I knew of someone. So now I was being invited back to Toronto to do a national network show that sounded worthwhile when the producer told me what it was about. It seems that there was definitely a problem among the youth in Canada and this particular program had an audience for the 15-35 year olds. The problem was depression and it seemed to be coming on in epidemic proportions by the amount of anti-depressant prescriptions that were being written. The producer thought that a show on NDEs might help. Oh! And could I bring some other "NDErs" with me.

"Hum" I told him. "It's been a long time. I guess I could call my friends from my support group up in Connecticut. How many do you want?"

Luckily he already had three or four and wanted one more. As he said one more, I remembered something about Carole once mentioning, although very briefly and almost shyly, that she had had an experience. I remembered a little of it but also remembered that she was cautious about revealing too much, but I knew she felt she had been with God.

"I'll ask around and get back to you. I know one young woman in her early 30's but I don't know if she will be willing." I said.

"That's the age group we are targeting. Tell her besides airfare, we'll put the two of you up at a top hotel with a five star restaurant and a chauffeur driven limousine --wherever you want to go."

"I laughed as I said, "With that offer -- if she can't I'm sure I'll find someone! But how cold is it now in Toronto?"

"Dress warm! I won't tell you how cold it is here if you're coming from Atlanta!" And we both chuckled as we hung up.

I called Carole and asked her to meet me for coffee. There was a *Caribou Coffee* shop in the middle for both of us and it became *our* place for coffee over the years. I sat there with my decaf watching her wave through the window and come in. She kind of "pranced" over to the counter and got herself a latte. As she sat down I asked, "Boy, you're looking chipper today. What's up?"

"I don't know but I feel good. I think your healings must be helping and when you called and asked me here I thought, "Yes! I could use a 'Barbara fix!'"

We both laughed and I said, "A Barbara fix! Is that what I am?"

Carole looked deeply into my eyes and said, "I've realized that I feel better when I'm with you. And, if I haven't been with you in a while-- I need a fix!!"

"What a perfect lead in." I said, "How'd you like to take a trip with me-- all expenses paid... to Toronto. Airfare, chauffeur and limo, 5 star restaurant in a fabulous hotel. We go next Tuesday morning and come back Wednesday evening."

Carole's face was wide with excitement and caution at the same time. "What do we have to do? Boy, I would love to get away. In fact, this morning I was praying for a get-a-way."

"Hum! Another synchronicity," I said. "I've been asked to do a TV show by a producer that I've done previous work with and I remember him as being all right. He wants me as "the expert" and he has three NDErs coming on but asked if I know one more I could bring. You told me you had an experience although I don't remember too much about it. But if you've had one, you qualify and we could have fun. What do you say? We'll be under stress for one hour while they film and we'll have fun for the other 35 hours. It will be an adventure!"

Carole looked pensive for a few seconds. Then she answered, "But Barbara, I didn't die."

"Carole." I answered, "I didn't die either."

"Yeah" She said. "But I wasn't even hurt. The car was spinning out of control and I thought I was going to die. You should have seen the car. It was totaled, but we walked away unhurt."

"Sounds like a near-death experience to me. I've heard several like that. Your experience is real as long as it is your experience! No one can tell you it's not an 'NDE' because you didn't get hurt. Did it change you? Can you remember it vividly? Can you remember dreams that happened that long ago?"

She thought for a while. "I remember it like it just happened and I was 19 at the time so it's been over 12 or 13 years. And, yeah, it changed me. I feel, I mean I felt and still feel like God is with me all the time. For sure I was with God."

And so I answered, "And that's what the youth of Canada need to hear. If they're depressed, then someone like you-- who is young like them-- can tell them what it was like to be with God. And me -- I'm the 'expert' so I'll validate you." And I laughed at the thought of being an expert. I never felt like an expert. I guess that's what the NDE really does to us. I told Carole that I feel more like a human being who stepped out of time for 'a second' and was in eternity with God. She and I agreed that once you've had an experience like we've had, no one is an expert, and no one is higher or lower than anyone else.

We fell into silence. My heart was bursting forth with gratitude for the gift of this young woman/old Soul coming into my life. This relationship that was deepening between the two of us was so rare, so incredibly rare that I knew her presence was allowing me to 'grow' my Soul beyond what I could have imagined-- and I knew she was being given the same gift. We now had shared experience and vulnerabilities that we openly acknowledged: this experience with Carole, another spiritual seeker felt joyous and expansive, and rare, incredibly rare.

We broke our silence- first agreeing that we came here from spirit and now we're trying to experience what it is to be human --and we needed to share that-- and then someday--we smiled-- we'll go back again to spirit.

We both acknowledged that we *needed* to go to Toronto and tell our NDEs to anyone who wanted to know about them. I remember us giggling and then bursting into joy. I remember thinking how we really saw each other.

Our friendship continued to reveal deeper and higher, sadder and funnier, spiritual and grosser parts of each other. And this wonderful two way mirror that we formed-- continues even today-- beyond the veil that separates us -- only by this otherwise temporal and temporary illusion.

Carole had her hair cut the day before we left. She hated it. Our flight had to be re-routed because of a winter storm. We arrived late. Our luggage was at another terminal so we had to take an airport bus to the next terminal and then another bus back. The driver and limo were waiting and we arrived late at the hotel-- at the time we were supposed to leave for the studio. We ran to our room and instead of the leisure rest and dressing period we had planned, we opened our suitcases and grabbed our clothes. Instead of the long bubble bath we had each planned in our separate rooms, we grabbed a wash cloth and quickly sponged ourselves. The fun part was that when we checked in we decided we didn't want separate rooms. We were rushing but we both took the time to confirm to each other that it would be more fun to be together in one room. So we went running back to the elevator and down to the front lobby where the young, handsome driver looked worried. We were once again in the stretch limo -- only to get caught up in heavy rush hour traffic. It took us almost an hour to get to the studio.

The producer and several young interns anxiously greeted us. They took us to the green room where there was a buffet set up and we helped ourselves to a plate of food. Because I was 'the expert' I had my own dressing room and as I was escorted to it I invited Carole to join me. We had been introduced to the other NDErs who were as nervous as we were and I knew at this point that it is much better to be alone in a little dressing room then to try to make light conversation. Carole and I got in the room and she again looked at her hair and said she needed to find a new hairdresser. I thought she looked beautiful. And I knew that she was fast becoming like one of my kids. What I didn't know yet was that she was thinking of me as the 'good mother' she felt she had never had.

"Let's pray." I suggested. "Let's ask Spirit to come through us-- to use us to help these young people who are depressed."

We sat facing each other and held hands. We prayed silently for a while and then Carole suddenly pulled away her hands. She was dripping with perspiration. "Whew!" she said. "I'm so hot. I'm burning up. Did you feel that? Barbara, you are really something."

"It's not me!" I said. "It's Spirit!" (And I truly meant that. It's never 'me' when I pray and ask Spirit to come through. I get out of the way and Spirit works through me.)

I wasn't sure what Carole's response was going to be. Maybe this was all too much for her. Maybe I never should have disclosed this side of me.

There was a knock at the door. I opened it and there was the producer with a beautiful young woman who was the host of the show. She was flushed and appeared shaken. She had something she needed to tell me.

"I can't believe it. I was in my dressing room reading the script and I started to pray for this show. I looked up toward the ceiling and near the vent... you know, the vent for the heat... I saw angels flying around. I've never seen angels before. I just had to tell you. I know you study these things. I can't believe it. I'm so happy. Thank you for being on the show."

Then she and the producer left.

Carole, looking a little stunned, said: "Boy, is this going to be a show!"

"Are you all right?" I asked.

"Oh yeah! Barbara. I'm fine. I'm all right. But.... this is all so amazing." And suddenly, an intern was there taking Carole to make up. I was taken in five minutes later.

LIVE ON TAPE

We watched the first three guests on the TV monitor. The first young woman was a recovering drug addict. She had lived a painful life before her near-death experience. She was a mother of two and had given up her children because of her addiction. She said she wanted a better life for them than she was capable of giving them. She said that she knew she had wanted to die. Then one night, without being on any drugs, she accidentally fell off a balcony. She had a profound near-death experience and after that never used drugs or alcohol again. She was working hard to get her life back together in a healthy way.

The next two guests were on together. They were a mother and her 15 year old daughter who had been in a terrible auto accident. Both told of their injuries. The young girl with scars over one eye had several plastic surgeries and a few more to go. They both had profound near-death experiences during the accident and again a few days after while in the Intensive Care Unit. While they were still talking, Carole was taken into the studio by an intern. I went into the green room and sat alone and watched her on the monitor.

The young woman host announced her by saying: Now meet Carole. She says she will never forget her near-death experience-- especially her conversation with God. Thank you for being here today.

Carole: Thanks for having me.

Host: When did you have your near-death experience?

"About 13 years ago."

"How did it happen?"

"I was in a car with my friend. She was driving and the car started veering off the road and we were heading toward a telephone pole. All of a sudden everything went totally into slow motion. I saw the telephone pole coming at us. And thought I was going to die and said 'Gee, life is kind of short but it was sweet.' And a whole life review went past my eyes of different periods of my life. I saw myself as a young infant being taught to walk and various other images which I can't remember now what they all were but it made total sense to me then-- my whole meaning of my life and what had happened in my life. Then, there was a very bright light -- the brightest white light you could imagine. You would think it would be blinding but I could look straight into it. I thought it was the most beautiful thing that I'd ever seen. And I realized that it was God and at first it looked like the face of Jesus and then I realized that suddenly it was someone like in a throne -- like God. And then I thought to myself, 'Wait a minute, maybe this is female.' The form kept sort of changing. And there were a lot of white bubbles around as angels. They were angels but not like you think of an angel with wings. They were just floating beautiful bubbles. And I had a voice in my head which was male and I remember thinking 'that's so interesting that God is male and female at the same time.' But the message I got was, 'Don't worry about yourself. You'll be fine. Help other people.'"

"So you're seeing a God-like figure that seems to be changing before you. When you say you hear a voice, I mean -- get descript with us. What is it? Is it a low hollow voice -- is it your voice -- is it a familiar voice?"

"It wasn't an audible voice. It was like -- psychic -- psychically put into my head. But it seemed male to me. But you couldn't hear it. It was like a message was just beamed at me."

"Now, did you remember all this as it was happening? Did you acknowledge it or was it after the fact?"

"Absolutely, I acknowledged it. Time seemed to stop for me. This all happened before we hit the pole. We actually knocked the telephone pole over which doesn't usually happen. Your car ends up wrapped around the pole. We knocked the pole over. The car was completely crashed to where we were sitting. And we were not hurt at all."

"What about the images of different events in your life?"

"I don't really recall all of them. I remember learning to walk and they happened in a series of all different ages. But now I don't remember what all the images were."

"Did they have a message? Was it specific? I mean, was it all the times you were bad? Was it all the times you were..."

"No. It was more about the meaning of my life and why I was there in this life. What I'm to do. I didn't have a very happy childhood so a lot of it made sense to me and it was okay. I was able to look at it and... It made sense to me now why these things happened."

"Forgive everyone?"

The panel of guests all nodded their heads and said, "Yea."

An audience member spoke next. "Hi, my question is to Carole. When you told you're friends and family about this experience-- how did they start treating you after that?"

"I didn't really tell a lot of people about this. First of all I was worried that people would think I was crazy. You know, you go around telling people you saw God and it doesn't usually get received that well. And I also didn't really know this was a near-death experience. I never considered it that. It was more of my life flashed before my eyes and I would describe that part to my friends. And I would ask, 'Have you ever had that happen to you?' And they're like 'No.' And I didn't know to call it that till recently really when I started learning about what a near-death experience is. But the God part I left out. I had fear of people thinking I'm nuts."

"You talk about here a near-death experience. Is it fair to call it a near-death experience if you're not near death? The other three people here were in a coma and they said they had an out of body experience. For you this is a moment where you're visually flashing through your life. Is there a difference between the two?"

"Well, I feel blessed that I am alive. I mean, to have knocked the telephone pole over and if anyone could see the car and I didn't have a scratch on me. When we actually felt the car stop, we looked at each and thought "Are we actually still alive?" I feel very blessed that I'm here. And almost, maybe I should have died but I really feel I have angels around me.

"So you all feel like it wasn't your time? There's a reason why you are here today. There's a reason why we are all here today."

An audience member asked, "It seems as though all the experiences so far have either involved head trauma or drugs and I was just wondering like as a general question to all of you-- your using LSD or other drugs, have you had any serious flashbacks before the near-death experience."

Everyone on the panel answered, "I wasn't on any type of drug when it happened." Someone offered, "I've never taken drugs in my life." And then a voice said, "I was sober ten months when the accident happened."

The host asked, "Carole, are you afraid of dying?"

"Not at all, I think it is a beautiful and peaceful experience. I felt very loved and I mean I had fear at first and all fear was removed. And I just felt like, 'Gosh. I really thought that I would be around longer" and I had more to accomplish. But I was not scared and its very loving... you just feel love around you and no fear at all."

And then they broke for several commercials.

The host came back on and said, "Today's guests say they have had a near-death experience that changed their lives. Now meet today's expert, Barbara Harris Whitfield, author of *Spiritual Awakenings: Insights of the Near-Death Experience and Other Doorways to Our Soul.* Barbara, welcome to the show. Now you have had your own near-death experience, and when did that happen."

"It happened in 1975 when I was 32 years old. I was suspended in a Stryker-frame circle bed after spinal surgery. It was catastrophic spinal surgery and I couldn't move. The bed moved me. I lived like that for a month. About the third day after surgery, I started to die. Now, I had been an atheist and if I would have heard any of this I would have never believed it. But the next thing I knew I was out in the hallway and I thought 'well this is very strange. If they catch me out here I'm going to get into trouble because I'm supposed to be suspended in that bed.' And I moved back into the room and I saw my body lying there. I felt totally peaceful, totally calm-- better than I had ever felt in my life. So I hung out with 'her' for a while. It certainly wasn't me. I was up near the ceiling. And the next thing I knew, I was in a tunnel. I couldn't call it a 'tunnel' at the time but later when I became a researcher, I realized that 'tunnel' is the best word.

"And then my grandmother, who had been dead for 14 years, came and wrapped her arms around me and pulled me into her. And together we re-experienced the 19 years we were here together on this Earth. It was wonderful...

"And, then it happened again a week later. I had a life review as the others here have talked about. I had a classic life review."

"Did this take you through different events that have happened in your life?"

"It felt like it took 32 years and God was holding me. Together we were re-experiencing my life and I was getting all this information about my life and I could hear myself saying, 'No wonder! No wonder!' I was learning so much."

"What were you learning about yourself as you were seeing these images?"

"I was learning about the abuse I had received as a child. I had numbed out completely. I think that was part of being an atheist. I had numbed out because of all the pain in my childhood. I was experiencing the pain again but I was also experiencing my mother's pain and my father's pain-- why they were the way they were. And, I was realizing that we are all children of God and we all have our pain. But we are really here to love each other. We are all here to learn how to heal from our pain and learn to love ourselves."

"So you found forgiveness?"

"Absolutely. But not in a way that I understood forgiveness before. I let go of all the pain I had been holding onto because of my abuse. I could love my parents, too. I always had and always will. But I also knew that they weren't 'off the hook.' They need to deal with what they had done and probably will in their own life review."

"Have you ever said to yourself, 'Hold on here. There has to be a reason. There has to be a medical reason why this happened. It can't be spiritual.'"

"Well, that's why I went into the research. I wanted to find a reason. I couldn't use the word God for years. The word just choked in my throat till I saw the movie Star Wars and they talked about the 'Force' -- because I knew I had been with a *Force* or an energy. And I went into *medical* research. I did research at the University of Connecticut Medical School for six years. I wanted to know what this is-- and *it is* brain chemistry! It is all those hard nuts and bolts things that some people say when they don't want to believe us. But just like you can explain a radio because a radio has a logical explanation-- this also had a broadcast. Yes, our brain is a radio that picks up a broadcast-- but we can't explain the broadcast."

"Can you help us out a little more here. We hear these stories or experiences from everyone who comes up. And we hear snickers and we see the body language that's saying 'Oh!, Come On! Get Real!' What can we do? I mean, we are seeing more and more of this."

"Because more and more of 'this' is happening. There's more of this. It is becoming more and more prevalent. You know, before mine, I would have never believed anybody. I might have been one of the people who snickered. But as this is happening more and more I think it is going to become easier for other people to have these experiences and not near-death. You don't have to nearly die-- that's why I wrote *Spiritual Awakenings*. I give 14 triggers in that book and only one is near-death. There are many different ways to have this experience."

Then, we paused for a commercial break.

The host started the next segment saying, "Now Barbara, just before the break we talked about near-death experiences and the stages. Maybe you can talk some more about the stages and what triggers it."

"Well, an incredible sense of peace is usually the first. And then we talk about an out-of-body experience, being above our bodies looking down. Moving through a tunnel, seeing the Light, moving into the Light, feeling like you *are* the Light, coming out onto the other side where there is usually a beautiful landscape where you know if you cross over a barrier you won't be able to come back. And then the coming back, sometimes, the life review but only in about 23% of the cases.

"There are other triggers. You don't have to be near-death. Bottoming out from addiction, people who are getting off of drugs or alcohol are having light experiences. Bill W. starting Alcoholics Anonymous is a perfect example. He had a light experience in detox. People who meditate, people who are in intense prayer. I had one priest tell me a beautiful experience during his ordination. Women in childbirth, like Carole, they were in no way near actually dying but in childbirth spontaneously had this experience."

"Why do you think more and more people are interested in spirituality and there's more and more cases reported lately?"

"We're waking up! It's time! We are at the end of the 20th century and we're poisoning Mother Earth and there's a spirituality that's saying to us, 'Wake Up!' So a lot of us who are hearing this show or reading a book are waking up from that. And, we are being coaxed by Spirit so more and more of this is happening."

An audience member asked, "For those of you who have been on the other side, what does God look like? Or the Creator look like?"

Everyone on the panel answered at once, "There is no image. This is something that you feel. You feel it."

"Well then, how do you know it is God? Maybe it was somebody else who was there. Why do you think it was God?"

"You just know. There's this sense of amazing Unconditional Love, of Spirit. And this being doesn't have to forgive us because there is no forgiveness for what we have been. This being just loves us the way we are and have been. We've invented *sin* and *forgiveness.* This Being just overwhelms us with Unconditional Love. It's something that's very hard to explain."

Then the host asked, "Barbara, why is it that we as a society whether it's spirituality, experiences that we've had, out-of body experiences or something completely different-- that when it's not something that is happening everyday it's not something that everybody in society is experiencing-- that we are scared of it? And most likely, everybody will immediately say, 'It's not true! They're lying!' It's all negative things. Why is that?"

"This is our natural birthright, to be spiritual beings. We are spirit. We were spirit before we came into this body and we are going to be spirit again when we leave. Our societies, our religion, our education, our entire system the way it is set up -- keeps us in what we call the 'left hemisphere' of our brain. What we are talking about here are 'right hemisphere' experiences that we all deserve to have."

"So if you weren't religious before-- has this brought you to be religious again?"

"To be spiritual, not to be religious. Religion is a brand name. Spirituality is Generic...that we all are spirit."

Then the show was over. Carole and I hugged the host. We hugged the producer and a few interns. We hugged the other people on the panel and then we were back alone together in the limo.

"Whew!" Carole said, "That was surreal! I couldn't believe the set when I got out there under the lights. The colors were amazing and the people... I've never been on this side of the camera before. I don't think I want to be again either. I like editing. This 'live show' business is tough. And, I don't know how I came across. Did I sound dumb?"

"No, no." I answered. "You were really good. But I'll tell you-- from years of experience-- we really never know how we are until we get a copy of the show and that will take weeks because they're not showing it right away. And then, I never like the way I look or even what I said. We have to move so fast on live shows that we never get to say all the things we wanted to or say them the way we wanted to. But you were just fine. .. And for your first time, it's great that it's here in Canada because if you don't like it-- you don't have to show it to anyone. It really hurts when it's shown locally and everyone sees it and I've said something really stupid. That has happened. But let's not think about that right now. I was told there is a five star restaurant in our hotel and we are being treated by the network. So, let's go!"

DINNER WITH CAROLE

Twenty minutes later we were being guided to a table in the hotel restaurant. It appeared to be small, intimate and I wondered how such a small restaurant could be five star. It seemed like we were the only customers because the maitre'd was always with us or nearby, dropping in. He was older and his eyes danced when he looked at us. Our waiter seemed to really appreciate two women coming in so late and he treated us like we were royalty. And then there was the wine steward and several assistants to the waiter. There were many mirrors to make the restaurant look bigger--dim chandeliers, big arm chairs, little candle lit lamps on each table-- the colors were dull hues of pinks, mauves and purples. Huge vases filled with fresh flowers repeated the colors over and over.

I looked at Carole across the candle lit table. "Carole, you are glowing!"

She answered with a giggle, "It's all the make up they piled on us. And I'm flushed from the whirlwind of it all."

"Carole, you are pretty!" I insisted with a smile.

She answered at first logically, "It's this room. This place. The lighting. Actually... it's quite magical. We haven't even had any wine and I can feel it. Can you feel it, Barbara?"

"Yes, Carole. I can feel it. It's also the 'rush' that we can get from doing a television show. I'm sure we were pumping out endorphins like crazy. That's all true. But you know, I don't think I've ever sat alone with you in a restaurant with candle light and you look like an angel."

The wine steward agreed as he poured our wine.

Carole leaned over to speak quietly. "I used to be pretty. I could show you pictures when Alex and I were dating. But now, you know, since I remembered those horrible times from my childhood, my skin has broken out. You can see the scars. I developed cystic acne just like my dad. Did I tell you my father has scars from acne too. So every time I have looked in the mirror for the last few years-- all I see is my dad's skin."

"Yes, I can see the scars. But you are *still* pretty, Carole! And didn't you mention having them removed? Then you won't see them and you will see how pretty you are. Right now you have the look of an angel or maybe a pixie. If your legs were longer we could call you "Tinkerbell!" And we both laughed.

Carole said, "I'm taking this strong medication that the dermatologist gave me. I'll take it for a year and then he is going to do dermabrasion on my face so hopefully, the scars will go away. But for now it's just these pills I take. And look at my nails."

Carole showed me three nails that were loose and eventually would fall off. She said, "That's from the medication to help clear up my skin."

"Well, honey." I answered, "I think a few nails are worth losing if it means you can eventually look in the mirror and see your beautiful face instead of focusing on some acne scars."

"Yeah, and then I can get pregnant. I have to finish this medication first before I can.

"Barbara, you talked a little bit on TV about your child abuse. I thought I heard you mention once before that more people who were abused as kids have spiritual experiences. Is that true? Is that me?"

"Oh, Carole, that's you, and a lot of us. We had such painful things done to us as children and in order to survive we left those scenes." I watched Carole's eyes open wide and she nodded yes.

I continued, "Psychology and psychiatry calls that 'dissociation' and treats it as pathology. Dissociation is a defense mechanism that child abuse victims used to survive. Now we take our 'ability' to dissociate and use it to become totally absorbed-- and then transcend to other realities. My friend and colleague Kenneth Ring, Ph.D. showed that in his research. It's as though we turn away from this reality and become absorbed in alternate realities. And, some of us do it easily. Ken calls it our 'compensatory gift' that we *earned*!' I'm not saying that the only way to learn this is through child abuse-- I have seen artists and musicians who easily do it too and they where never abused."

"I dissociate when I'm focused," Carole answered, wide eyed.

"I know you do. I watch you sometimes. I watch you when you are doing something artful and I watch you become totally absorbed in it. Then I watch the 'muse' coming through you and your art becomes playful."

"You really do see me, Barbara. You really can." Carole said shaking her head, "And, I can see you. I can see who you are-- your depth and your beauty. And I'm so grateful to have you in my life."

"Yes, Carole." I answered. "And, I'm grateful to have you in my life. You and your experiences have filled you with Unconditional Love that spills over to everyone, including all your pets."

And we both smiled as we thought of the menagerie of animals she had left for Alex to care for in this extraordinary 36 hours we were away.

"One more thing," I said, "All of us who are in recovery had a variety of reasons. And a big one is-- we don't like ourselves. We don't think we are pretty or nice or all the other messages that our parent's abuse and neglect gave us. We didn't see the love in our parents faces when they looked at us because their own addictions, wounds and other traumas takes away their ability to like or to love themselves so they can't give us love either. And we grow up with that memory of the way they looked at us. I used to call it 'my mother's dirty looks.' I'd look in the mirror and see my mother's look in *my* face. I called that, 'not pretty.' But 'pretty' had nothing to do with it. I was looking at my undeserved shame and sadness. I was a sad child and a sad adult until I worked on my own healing.

But we're not just abuse survivors-- you and me. We know we're spirit. We know we are children of God. We can, if we choose, look in the mirror and see God's love the way it was shown to us. You're not just Carole, the abuse survivor over here and Carole the near-death experiencer over there. You're not just Alex's wife here, and a great film editor over there. Being Alex's wife and being in the 'Industry' overlap all the time. You are all those things in one *whole* package so let the light of God's love shine on all the scars. Not just your face, but the scars in your heart and your mind. Let God's light help you become whole again. Your parents couldn't give you the love, but now *you* and God can give it to you.

"I feel what you are telling me. I feel different. Something is changing inside of me. It's like... Telling about my experience with God in front of all those people tonight... I'm not hiding that part of me anymore. I want to tell the world. Oh God!! I'm starting to feel.... I don't have words for it but I believe this is what I have been praying for forever!" And she looked me deeply in the eyes and pleaded, "This doesn't have to go away. Does it?"

"No sweetheart. It will only get bigger and better!"

CHAPTER 4

BRINGING IN THE LIGHT

And somehow, on the plane-- and then as we drove home-- I could feel a difference in the way it felt to be with Carole. We weren't so heavy in our conversations. We weren't talking about the darkness as much anymore... Carole and I discovered each other again, no longer as victims of childhood trauma, but as spiritual human beings. Our conversations turned more toward the Light-- toward the goodness of man. Something had shifted...

We had changed our outlook from the darkness to the Light. Carole even helped me write a piece for the new book I was working on-- *Final Passage: Sharing the Journey as this Life Ends.* In this book I told several stories of people who I sat with as they died. These stories illustrate that total 'non-interference' makes way for Spirit, for God, to move in and help the person die with dignity and grace. Through stories, I explain the spiritual nature of death and dying.

My editor had asked me to tell the story of my near-death experience again. My parents (my mother, a prescription drug addict, and my father an enabler of my mother's disease) had both died. So I decided this time I wanted to tell my near-death experience in a deeper way. I was ready to talk more about my experience of abuse and how God's love can move us through the pain.

I shared all my stories with Carole as I wrote them and when I started reading my NDE to her she got excited and made beautiful descriptive suggestions. Curled up on one of her sofas with the manuscript in my hand, I stopped and listened to her each time-- then added everything she said about what it was like to be with God. I remember reading it back to her when we were finished. The atmosphere was as soft as the circle of candles glowing around us. And we both had tears twinkling on our cheeks and we were softly saying, "We got It! We got It!' She cheered and burst into giggles. Her laughter was contagious. The lightness of her being spilled over onto me.

I became aware of a new sense of something coming from Carole. Sometimes light seemed to emanate from her face. Even when she left the room-- I could still feel her presence. It was becoming stronger. As she freed herself from the bondage of her past -- her real self started coming out and as it did she began almost to glow because the light was radiating from within her-- not from an outside source. As the years went by, looking back on all this now, it was as though it was easier to see Carole as a beautiful angel or "Tinkerbell" type fairy that had come down into a human form. She still fought all the same human mind tricks as the rest of us. But as she uncovered each new answer to make her life easier, and inch her way toward healing and wholeness she embraced joy and compassion for herself and all of us.

I also noticed that when we were together we were able to put our egos aside and achieve an authentic sense of "joining." We could say things very spiritual and very deep. And we could also say hilarious stuff. Our humor could be clever or gross or even outside the "box." We could get outside the "box" and discuss our egos in a way that would relate to our childhood abuse and how it was still spilling over into our lives now. It was as though we were in this "zone" and it was almost palpable as a "presence" that we were in and also radiated from us. We talked about it as "spirit" and I called it "grace" because it felt like a gift. Sometimes it even felt sacred and most often it was joyful.

MOTHER'S DAY

We met Carole and Alex before 8 o'clock in the morning and were standing in line by 8:30 at the Emory University campus to see the Dalai Lama-- us and 4,000 others. We sat in a big gym but we could see him and were happy to just be in his presence. After, we had brunch back at Carole and Alex's and even though Carole was happy from seeing the Dali Lama -- she still had to show me a poem she had written about her mother before we came that morning. She said the feelings were just 'oozing up' and she had to let them come out. I walked out on the deck and read it.

Mother's Day

(5/10/98)
Today is Mother's Day
And all I can think of
Is how sad I am for you.
For all you have missed...
And still continue to.
You sacrificed your babies
For the comfort of material goods,
You sold your Soul to the devil,
Your life based on 'shoulds'.
You slowly decompose
From the inside out,
Spirit so weak,
Full of self-doubt.
My heart weeps
For the mother you could be,
For the choices you've made,
For your lack of glee.

You've lived your life
With your eyes closed,
Always the 'victim'
Even though these are
The paths you chose.
I can only wonder how you feel today
Thinking of the children you threw away.
Not a card, flower or loving sentiment
From your grown babies who were heaven sent.
How could you turn your back on your most precious gift?
You're a lost Soul forever adrift.

I asked Carole if she was going to send this to her mother and she answered 'no.' She wanted no contact with them and was afraid if she mailed it to her -- it would start some kind of correspondence. I told her about a Native-American ritual of taking unmailed letters and burning them with sage or cedar while saying a prayer to send the message to Spirit to do whatever Spirit sees fit.

Carole and Alex had a fire pit in the back yard and a few minutes later we were praying and watching the smoke go up from the burning poem.

ATLANTA TV NEWS

Alex was working for an Atlanta television station as a producer. They were doing a piece for the evening news on healers. Alex called and asked if a crew could come over and film me. So I set up my massage table in our home office and as I was demonstrating healing and being interviewed, Carole sat and watched.

"This stuff is so amazing," She said, "And look at my hands. I know it works because you're helping me heal."

I answered, "Carole, it's not me. It's Spirit working through me. Anyone can do it. All it takes is the *intention* to want to help someone. You don't even have to believe in the energy. All you need is the *intention* to help someone."

"Really?" asked the interviewer. "Is that what I feel in the room? This room feels so good? Are you telling me it's Spirit I feel?"

"Yes. Every time we extend our self to help another or every time we need help ourselves-- all we need do is ask and Spirit is here. I pray before every healing that I do --for help from the Holy Spirit. That's what you are feeling in this room. I've done more healings than I can count here. It always feels good." I said. "It's a transpersonal power. 'Transpersonal' means it is beyond me. It's energy that comes through us from a Source beyond our personal energy. It's not something I or any *one* possesses. It's beyond any of us individually -- beyond the personal. We could say that it's the power of love because-- this Energy that we here in the Western World call 'The Holy Spirit,' 'Great Spirit' or 'Ruach ha Kadosh' -- in its emotional component feels like love.

THE CONFERENCE COMMITTEE AND THE HOLY SPIRIT

Ever since my research on this Energy at the University of Connecticut, I have been a board member of an International group of researchers who are looking at this Energy; in the Yogic tradition it is called 'Kundalini.' Our group is comprised of researchers who are physicians, psychologists, scholars, therapists and individuals interested in conducting and collaborating on research into spiritual states of consciousness and their relationship to energy. We call ourselves the 'Kundalini Research Network' (KRN).

Kundalini is a term used to describe the transformative spiritual energy/consciousness in human beings. When activated, it may be responsible for such diverse spiritually transformative events as healings, mystical experiences, inspired creativity and genius, near-death experience, some paranormal experiences, and a host of other physiological and psychological reactions.

One of the primary goals of KRN is to bring the findings of this research to the scientific and medical communities, to therapists and to people undergoing these energetic or Spiritual awakening experiences in order to facilitate and make more understandable this often complex and profound process.

Since its founding in 1990, the Network has welcomed interested individuals from around the world. It is not restricted to any religious tradition or spiritual discipline. The common thread is an interest in the scientific verification of this life force/spiritual energy phenomenon and a desire to make this information available to people from all backgrounds.

We meet annually to present new findings, review and plan research projects, collaborate on articles and meet others interested in this research. Here we present lectures and workshops from traditional, cross-cultural, and clinical perspectives.

I was president of the organization for 1998, and as such, I was chairing our annual Conference here in Atlanta. I had made a reservation at a beautiful retreat center about 20 minutes from our house. It was set on over 100 acres of forest with the Chattahoochee River running through it. Now, with a year count down until the conference, I was organizing my notes of what needed to be done and looking for a group of volunteers who could help me because my notes turned into a task list of five type written pages.

During these first planning months, I sent out letters of invitation to speak to the members of the board of KRN and friends, associates and colleagues I had met along my own path. It was exciting to hear from people I hadn't talked to in years and when I did-- and they accepted my invitation-- I knew they had a piece to the puzzle although I wasn't exactly sure what that piece was or even what the puzzle looked exactly like. I only knew they were there for me as I traveled my own spiritual path and Spirit was helping me now to put this together in a way that I didn't need to understand.

Carole was the first to volunteer for my committee. She did all the computer graphics for the magazine advertisements, the brochures and the program. We spent hours each month at her computer. During this time, she quickly learned about each speaker. They were mainly physicians and professors of psychology, anthropology, philosophy and sociology. I invited spiritual teachers and healers, too. Carole was not only interested-- as the year wore on she sopped up the topics like a sponge. We spent hours talking about the speakers and the Energy and how it relates to the concept of the human Soul and Universal Spirit. I lent her books that I had by some of the speakers. I shared articles I had collected over the years. We sat and watched documentaries I had been involved in at the University.

Charlie and Alex would get involved in our discussions when we were all together. I had invited Charlie to be the opening speaker. Charlie's map of the psyche included not only our True Self and ego or false self, but also the Higher Self and Higher Power. When the True Self, Higher Self and Higher Power are connected in a free flowing relationship--Charlie called that relationship 'The Sacred Person.' This map would create a good overview for each speaker to be able to bring the audience back to the same ground as we heard all the different concepts from the diverse group of speakers.

That year, Carole also donated a great deal of time and energy editing a documentary project about the life of Mother Theresa, whom Carole loved and admired. The four of us shared many dinners with stimulating conversations ranging from the Holy Spirit, spiritual healings, Mother Theresa, The Dali Lama and even a living saint from India called Sai Baba. That year I brought Carole to one of the yoga classes I attended and after the first class she signed up for the series. She was beginning to understand the concept that our body is our temple and so she changed the way she and Alex ate. They continued smoking cigarettes, though. She said, "We just aren't ready to give it up."

IDEA FOR DOCUMENTARY

One day, as I walked in with my arms full of papers to be typed into Carole's computer, I told her I had thought of something really exciting for her and Alex but I wasn't sure how they would feel about it. I told her she and Alex should do a documentary on the conference. She looked like the cat who had swallowed the canary as she said, "Alex and I have been discussing that for a while and we were about to tell you we want to do it. We're going to shelve the documentary exposing the "falsies" for now and focus on showing people the light instead of the darkness. That's the best way we can help!!"

First, Carole composed a letter on their Celestial Productions stationary to send to all our speakers. She explained who she and Alex were and what they wanted to do. I added a paragraph explaining that Carole and Alex were good friends of mine and that I could vouch for their integrity, professionalism and reliability. We asked for books, articles, videos-- anything they could send that would help her to understand what their deepest concerns and messages were. Then, I watched her and Alex take all this in. I answered any questions I could. I loved what we were doing. I talked about the research I was involved in. I brought in the books I had read over the years when I was trying to figure out what was happening to me after my NDE-- about this Energy that took over my life and is my life. I saw It light up Carole's face. I saw It bring Carole and Alex closer. I saw It move Carole farther and farther away from the darkness of her memories of her childhood abuse. Looking back now I believe that this period could have been her real turning point. The scars of her childhood went back into the recesses of her mind, only now they had been aired out and exposed to the light so they were stored with less painful emotional content. On the other hand, the joy of the spiritual subject she was studying was filling her mind with wondrous and healing thoughts.

Ideas were bubbling over. Her energy brightened even more. Her eyes were sparkling. I could see Spirit working in her and eventually through her to help others. She and I would spend long hot summer afternoons on the deck, drinking sweet tea and watching hummingbirds at the feeder. Shannon, their dog would lie limply on the concrete dozing in the heat until a butterfly would wake her. The butterflies would dive bomb her nose and she would jump up and run around the yard trying to get them. Carole and my conversations became so meaningful, filled with suppositions of the way God's Energy works in our lives.

STAYING HUMAN

One afternoon, at the coffee shop, Carole was showing me a preliminary outline of the documentary. I wasn't understanding it because it was still vague so I was asking her lots of questions. She seemed a little distant and jumpy. I was about to ask her what was going on when she said,

"Wait a minute, Barbara. I don't understand-- what's going on? Skip the documentary for a few moments; I don't know what's going on!" She sounded vaguely disgusted. "I am having some uncomfortable feelings and I just can't get to them. But all this is so ... I don't know. Could it be because I'm reading Jennifer Freyd's book *Betrayal Trauma?* I feel like I want to scream."

"Say some more." I asked. "Can you say some more about being uncomfortable?"

I watched her 'feel around' inside herself for a few moments and then she said, "I'm angry, Barbara. I'm really angry at my parents. I can fill my head with all this wonderful stuff but it can't take away that gnawing feeling I still get."

"Have you ever tried to dump some of the anger experientially?" I asked, "Not just talking about it but screaming about it or doing anger bat work?"

"No! Well, maybe... I think I did some bat work years ago with my first psychologist. Yeah, I did something like that and I remember it helped." she answered.

Ten minutes later I was handing her our anger bat and arranging pillows on the floor. Carole grabbed the bat with a tremendously forceful determination. Carole beat the pillows over and over, screaming and demanding that her parent's abusive actions get out of her heart and her Soul. I couldn't believe her strength. She hit those pillows again and again. She worked extremely hard. When she was through she was sweating, crying and laughing all at the same time. "Whew," she said, "I feel a lot better!"

"Yeah, I can see you do. We can spend all of our lives studying lofty ideals. We can hope and choose to stay on the spiritual path but eventually our human feelings will bring us back here where we need to finish our work. Charlie and I call trying to stay with the spiritual and ignore our painful human feelings-- 'spiritual bypass.' It's good that you could identify something was troubling you and let the pillows have it."

"Yeah" she laughed in a hoarse voice, "Better the pillows then Alex!" and we laughed.

Then Carole picked up our copy of *Betrayal Trauma* that was on the book shelf behind her. Tears rolled down my face as Carole quoted Freyd, "These are not just molesters and co-molesters or enablers from the neighborhood who have no seeming obligation as parent figures. But when the parents molest and enable it to happen, when instead they are suppose to be protecting their child from abuse, neglect and other hurts. This is why it is a betrayal trauma. The parents betray the innocent child."

FIRST INTERVIEWS

Alex and Carole interviewed Charlie and me on camera about a month before the actual conference. They said that this would mean two less people to have to work into a three day shooting schedule. They set up all their equipment in our living room and interviewed Charlie first. I was glad Charlie was first because I pulled out my camera and photographed them in action.

Alex and another man set up lights, tested the sound and worked two cameras. Carole sat on a foot stool to one side of the cameras with head phones on. She asked Charlie questions that she had carefully thought out. He stared at her the whole time. In fact, every speaker did, including me. When the documentary would eventually be finished, although Carole is not seen on camera during the interviews and she carefully edited out her voice -- her presence is still huge. We are all staring at her. We are talking directly to her and she is innocence and intelligence mirroring us back.

They wanted to interview me outside because our neighborhood has huge beautiful trees. We started on the deck after much time and work setting up potted plants and lighting equipment and then it started raining. So we grabbed all the equipment and moved to our carport which gave us cover and still a beautiful background of trees. Of course, airplanes zoomed overhead, a flock of big black birds perched in our trees and screamed for quite a while and a neighbor blowing his leaves made us stop several times. But we kept a humorous attitude because we were excited. We officially started. We still weren't sure what the message was going to be but we knew Carole and Alex were holding this in their hearts and their incredible intellect-- so Spirit could move through to create something new, something that could help people know about this wonderful subject that was exploding in our hearts and our heads.

CHAPTER 5

THE KUNDALINI RESEARCH NETWORK'S 1998
CONFERENCE

Octber 14, 1998-- I pulled into Simpsonwood Conference and Retreat Center with my mini-van filled with all the paperwork and boxes of paraphernalia, books, etc. I had been planning this day for over a year. Passing the gates the speed limit was 15 miles an hour. The narrow road meandered and curved around in the peaceful old oak forest. I passed the beautiful old pristine chapel. Across the road was a huge swimming pool and a big meadow that was used for sports. Further on, set back among the trees, were old wooden buildings.

I leaned forward, over my steering wheel, to see the tall trees better. They were slowly turning into fall reds, oranges and yellows but not as much as I hoped. "Oh well. Just take a deep breath, and let these days be what Spirit wants them to be!"

I asked Spirit to bless everyone and give each participant and speaker everything they needed. I asked Spirit to bless Carole and Alex and the documentary. And I said a little prayer for myself to release all my overwhelming feelings.

I passed Brooks Complex, the building we were to be housed in. It was comparable to a Hilton with a little bit of childhood summer camp thrown in-- including big baskets of chewy chocolate chip cookies, juice and cocoa in gathering areas outside our rooms before bedtime. They also supplied urns of coffee and baskets of fruit and cookies near the meeting rooms in the conference center. Three sumptuous meals a day were served buffet style in a large pleasant dining room that invited us to go back and get more. Every meeting room, lounge and lobby had big windows looking out into the forest surrounding the buildings. The lobby and greeting area in the conference center not only had a fabulous view of a big deck filled with wood rockers overlooking the forest, but also a large stone fireplace and comfortable sofas and chairs that invited us to sit down in groups inside or out, depending on the weather. And the Chattahoochee River was 50 feet from the conference buildings. There was a scenic foot path following the river and circling the forest.

A MONTH BEFORE

I had brought Alex and Carole to Simpsonwood a month earlier to show them the location. They picked places to set up so each speaker would have a beautiful, natural background. There were benches looking out at the river and Carole practically danced with excitement from one spot to the next. Of course, if it rained they would be in "big trouble." And before we even completed the thought of what would happen if it rained, Doug Shepherd, the director of operations for Simpsonwood, appeared and volunteered a room in Brooks Complex for Alex and Carole to set up an indoor studio. He showed us a "typical" bedroom that contained two double beds and a desk plus dresser. His staff would clear a room like this one so that this film crew wouldn't have to work around the furniture. And Doug made sure it was just across the hall from their bedroom. I knew that on their own, Carole and Alex were going to a huge expense to rent all the equipment and hire extra people to help with the filming. Since she had helped so much with the planning of the conference, and because she and Alex were now "Media" people, KRN covered the expense of their room and board for the four days we were there. My friend Joanne Chambers was coming to the conference from Columbia, Maryland and volunteered to do the transcribing of the seventeen hours of interviews that came out of those three packed days.

I saw Michael walking from one building to the next. He worked and lived at Simpsonwood and also attended the class Charlie and I taught on *A Course in Miracles*. "Hi" he greeted me with a hug. I introduced him to Alex and Carole. I told him their plans to film a documentary during our conference and he generously offered to help them-- that included physically moving all their equipment. Then he invited us to stay for lunch and so we walked over to the conference center and Carole and Alex saw it for the first time. The front doors of the building are made of a large carved wooden relief sculpture of Christ with his hands opened wide to greet visitors. Alex slowly ran his hands over the doors. I reminded Carole and Alex that it didn't matter what we called the Energy we were gathering to study: "Kundalini," "Holy Spirit," "Ruach Ha Kadosh," or "Christ Consciousness" The name didn't matter. It was all one Energy. It was God's love for us--Only we humans give "It" a "brand name."

Carole reminded me that I said that when we did the TV show in Canada and then she told me how much she loved that statement about "brand names" and she knew she wanted to use it to start off the documentary. We agreed I would start my interview with the "brand names" sound bite. They now had Charlie and I thinking in terms of concise sound bites.

Alex was thrilled with the idea that he could help himself at a buffet table and go back for more. Being the "Jewish mother" that I am, I loved watching his six foot two frame filling his plate. Carole and I stood wide-eyed over the dessert table that had two different pies, a huge sheet cake and assorted sauces next to a soft ice cream machine and we said, "Oh Boy!!"

Carole and Alex mentioned over and over that this was almost surreal -- the grounds, the deeply carved wood doors with Christ extending his hands, the kindness of my friend Joanne, Doug Shepherd, Michael and KRN. They felt overwhelmed by everyone's generosity. Everything was coming together.

We joined hands before we started our meal and Alex said Grace: He said something about knowing God was present and working through all these people for things to come together. We could feel it. Then Alex in his beautiful deep voice-- half spoke half sang the words from the Phil Collins song *I can feel it coming in the air tonight.* He raised his volume and his eyebrows when he got to the part "I've been waiting for this all my life-- Hold on! Hold on!" Carole touched his shoulder and sang, "Me too. Me too."

As we ate they explained to me how everyone who works in television has their big dream-- a documentary they are going to do-- "someday." Everyone walks around dreaming about their own particular documentary subject. But now they, Carole and Alex -- Celestial Productions-- were actually *doing* it. Occasionally, they would have to pause and we were very quiet. They couldn't talk at all. I would watch their eyes wander out through the windows. At one point Carole jumped when her eyes fell upon a rooster that was pecking around under a bush. She and Alex laughed when I told them that chickens and roosters wandered the grounds.

Alex was quiet for a long time and then he said, "Simpsonwood has a magical quality about it. There are so many places to set up for the interviews and I can just see already how it's going to look-- or maybe I can't even imagine what is going to happen in front of the camera. This whole thing is taking on a surreal quality."

We were quiet driving home. I sat in the back and noticed that Carole and Alex's eyes would meet occasionally and they would smile knowingly to each other. I saw him take her hand once and tenderly look at her. I loved being with them.

When they dropped me off , I asked them to wait while I ran in and got my "amazing" vest that I had bought at an art gallery in Key West. It was made of two sheer layers of black mesh and amply suspended every few inches or so were golden three dimensional suns, moons and stars. I brought it out to Carole.

"Here" I said, "You might want to wear something celestial while you are asking the questions during the interviews."

"Oh, Barbara," Carole said. "This is wonderful. The whole thing is wonderful. I can't believe this."

She tried to thank me but I wouldn't or couldn't hear of it. This wasn't me. This was Spirit working through us... I just had the joy of watching "It."

So I told them what a wise documentary film maker had told me years ago when we completed a glorious half hour TV show he named *Back From Light*. "When we are working in the service of Spirit, everything seems to speed up. We have entered what feels like a Jet Stream--which can feel turbulent in the beginning.... But then eventually we move into the 'slip' A jet steam has a calm center called a 'slip' just like the 'eye' of a hurricane. When we move into the 'slip' we know we are working hard in service --but things take on a sense of calmness-- we move along smoothly, we have a great sense of playfulness and everything comes along seemingly arranged for by a Higher Will."

And I concluded, "*We are now in the 'slip!'*"

PRE-CONFERENCE AND CONFERENCE

The actual conference started Friday evening at 7:00. However, we had asked five speakers to do a one day "pre-con" (a one day workshop before the conference) on Thursday from 10 am to 4 p.m. So, many of us moved into Simpsonwood on Wednesday evening to attend the pre-cons on Thursday. Most of our board came in Wednesday evening and I remember standing in the greeting area of the conference center beaming as people from all over the world came in. Everyone was excited, laughing and hugging-- catching up on each others lives. And, as they entered, everyone was talking about the wooden doors with Jesus extending his hands.

"How did you find this place?" they asked me. And, "Oh Barbara! You've done a wonderful job. The conference packets are beautiful and so well organized." I smiled and said, "Thanks to that young woman over there named Carole." and nodded toward her. "She did all the computer graphics on everything! All I did was type the information into her computer.

"And she's the one that's going to interview you for the documentary. I'm working on this documentary with her and her husband, Alex. And I know it's going to be wonderful! I'll be there when Carole does the editing. Please don't have any hesitations when it comes to your interview. Just say what you want to-- what is in your hearts."

I glanced at Carole again and walked over. "Are you all right?" I asked. "You look tired."

She smiled and said, "Yeah, I am. We've carried stuff in all day and moved it around and around until we got it right. You've got to walk over with me to Brooks Complex and see our studio."

Five minutes later I was standing in the studio they had created in one day. "Oh! This is amazing."

They were beaming and exhausted. Then Alex said proudly, "And now the real work begins."

They worked non-stop for the next four days. Some speakers were interviewed outside with the river in the background. And several were interviewed in the studio they created for variation.

I attended the pre-con given by David Nowe. He led us in chants, meditation and prayer. I was called out occasionally to handle some kind of administrative problem but I still spent many hours with the 20 other participants as we experientially shared a strong sense of joy and peace. David is the founder and Spiritual Director of the 'God Realization Ministry' dedicated to awakening seekers to the direct experience of God. He travels extensively giving workshops and is a member of the Ministerial staff of the Unity Church. He is also owner of a video production company. For 8 years David lived and studied with Swami Muktananda, the renowned spiritual master from whom he received Divine Initiation. Since 1980, he has shared the special gift he received from his own master with many students world-wide. During our day together, David twice did a "laying on of hands" as it is called here in the West. In the East it is called "Shaktipat." The sense that the "receiver" gets ranges from a sense of peace and blessing all the way to losing consciousness and then awakening with a sense of being healed. I was grateful I had spent the day in David's workshop. The peace I received took me through the four days. I was definitely in the 'slip.'

I invited a Catholic Priest to begin the conference with a blessing. Then a Hindu prayer was given and finally a Native American Ritual.

Two speakers presented the first night, Dr. Bonnie Greenwell, from California and then a doctor from India. Some stayed after to chat. I was headed toward Brooks to get some sleep and I peaked into Carole and Alex's studio. Carole was drenched with perspiration and exhaustion. "I hope it's bedtime." I half asked.

And, just as she nodded, I saw David Nowe passing the door.

"David," I called and grabbed his arm. "Please, give these two kids whatever they need. They've interviewed all day and right after this they're going to sleep."

He nodded and talked about understanding having been in TV Documentary work himself. The three went off together and I watched them grab some milk and cookies off the cart and go into David's room.

The next morning at breakfast, Carole walked up to me with that glow in her face and twinkle in her eye. "Barbara, David was amazing. He blessed us, hands on and Oh! I'm not even sure I can talk about it yet."

"Don't" I answered. "Not now. We'll have plenty of time later. You have a great day-- lots of good interviews!"

The speakers were mainly affiliated with academic and research institutions. Before their on-camera interviews with Alex and Carole-- I again reassured them because I knew that many of us had been "burnt" before by media people. It's one thing to be interviewed live on camera. We still felt some sense of control when the interview was live. But doing documentaries or any interview that can be edited-- left us at the mercy of the producer and editor.

The media often sensationalizes or twists what we say to their own biases and that had happened to me more than once. In the early 80s, near-death experiences were considered material for Halloween shows and there were a few times I was embarrassed to walk into the university because some TV show had made me look foolish with their editing or their host's comments. Only once did I have a producer call and apologize. This was about a filmed interview done at the New York studio of one of the big 'three' networks and was to be shown on a well known national morning program. The interviewer, who is also well known, had said to me during the interview, "I have absolutely no context for what you are saying. My religious background allows no room for any of this!" The producer apologized over the phone the next day and asked if she could send another crew to my office at the university. They filmed the whole interview again. But that considerate producer was the exception. The rest of the time we had at best a 50-50 chance of their making us look foolish. I wanted my colleagues who were being interviewed by Carole and Alex to know that they were different.

I was surprised and then delighted when I realized that Carole and Alex's interviews were adding incredibly to the open heartedness of the conference. They were opening each speaker to their deepest truth which in turn brought a huge sense of joy because we were being given a chance to express ourselves. The speakers in turn radiated this joyful openness to the audience. I didn't quite understand what was going on until I saw Judith Miller after her interview. "Oh, Barbara," she said with moist eyes and a flushed face, "Those two are so young and adorable. They're so filled with idealism. And Carole's questions were well thought out-- and then Alex would jump in with more great questions. He was not only following along, and understanding what I was saying -- but he could take us to an even deeper level with his questions. Those two are wide open and wonderful!"

I smiled and answered, "We're still not sure what the documentary is going to conclude but we know in our hearts that we're being guided ... I've watched those two take high-intellectual concepts and bring them down to something that can be understood by the heart. Oh and by the way, Judy, Do you know you're beaming?"

"I know! I can feel it!" and she started to laugh as she said, "And, I'm probably going to be fired for what I've said but -- I don't care. It's time I spoke out for what I believe. I come to these conferences and speak and get so much validation from all the other people in our field. Then I have to go back to a mental health system that treats spirituality as "religious ideation" and labels that as mental illness. It's time we all speak out!"

"I think we are, Judy. I think we are."

When I watched the interviews a few weeks later, I couldn't stop crying. Each one of us starts out being highly academic and intellectual... And, somewhere around 10 minutes or so, there's a shift in all of us as Spirit moves in and... we change. My shift was obvious. My friend, Jyoti, who is a Native American Minister still makes me cry when I think of the moment when she said, "God's not scary... We are." She and her husband Russell Park, a clinical psychologist, have a spiritual community in northern California. They talked about their experiences living in and leading such a community-- trying to live in a better way. She also talked in her interview about her own spiritual awakening and how she suddenly realized that she didn't like where she had chosen to 'sit.' And with tears in her eyes, she said, "our children grow tall in body, but we aren't attending to the growth of their spirits." I knew when I saw her after their interview that what we had prayed and asked Spirit for had happened and much more than we understood yet. The whole conference took on a quality that I didn't need to understand. I just walked through it with a sense of fullness, peace and intense gratitude.

THE BIGGER LINE

Just before the printing of the conference program, Bonnie Greenwell, a founding member of KRN, sent me a new book by a professor from New York Medical College, Lawrence Edwards. I was enthralled by his writing and after finishing his book called him to ask if he would speak at the conference. Even though it was quite late to ask, he accepted and sounded as excited to be coming as I was to be asking him. Now I was watching him sit down in the dining room with his dinner tray. I walked over and asked if I could join him.

"Yes but you'll have to excuse me if I am a little far away. I was just interviewed by the documentary people... and, frankly... they are delightful."

Lawrence Edwards is tall, 6 foot 4 and has a beautiful voice. I know part of his appeal comes from his high intelligence and especially his humility. The talk he had given that morning was as inspiring as his writing. I understood his amazement after being interviewed by Carole and Alex, and I felt lucky to have caught him right after the interview so I could sit alone with him and listen to his comments. He was staring off into the distance and smiling. "They filmed me sitting among huge trees with the river behind me and the river was filled with sun light... There were even ducks swimming behind me as they filmed. I could feel Spirit surrounding us and then as we were ending they asked me to say anything I wanted -- one message I would like them to deliver..."

I sat there smiling as he talked. Then briefly I told him Alex and Carole's story about everyone who works in the television industry having this dream of *their own* documentary-- and how Alex and Carole's dream of their first documentary was going be to expose the parents who banned together against their children who disclosed that they were sexually abused by them.

"When we met Carole and Alex they were vehement about telling the truth about these people. Then, when I started planning this conference, we got the idea at the same time and their plans shifted to doing a documentary with the speakers from this conference."

I finished with, "Carole and Alex are remarkable. And I'm glad I've been able to be a part of their shift from wanting to go after those dark people to creating a documentary about... about what we have to say!"

Lawrence sat silently for a time. Then he said, "They drew the bigger line!"

There was a long pause between us.

"What?" I asked.

Lawrence said. "Alex and Carole drew the bigger line. They are choosing not to engage in -- or attack-- the smallness of some other group's line. Instead they are choosing to work toward bringing others to the awareness of the Infinite. Carole and Alex have decided to draw the bigger line!"

"Where did you get that?" I asked.

"From the writings of Swami Ram Tirth.[2] He would give a group of students a challenge by drawing a line on the blackboard and asking them to make it smaller without touching it or erasing it in any way. After a few vain attempts and everyone giving up, he would go to the board and draw a longer line above the other, making it obviously shorter.

"When we bring the fullness of the Self, the Truth, the Light and Love of the Divine into our consciousness and into our life, the relative smallness of so many other things becomes apparent...." He concluded, "Carole and Alex have decided to draw the bigger line!"

"Wow!" I said. And now I was the one who couldn't talk...

Later in the week, after the conference was over and things quieted down, Charlie and I were visiting with Carole and Alex. We were delighted when they told us what Lawrence Edwards had said at the end of his interview. Alex was putting a cigarette in his mouth and froze when Lawrence leaned in very close to Alex's ear and with great force and determination said, "You should stop that. Why don't you **quit** now?" Within a few days Alex and Carole quit smoking. Alex said, ""We both had tried quitting before but this time it seemed, well, easy. It was strange. Lawrence sort of

---

[2] Swami Ram Tirth was a great proponent of non-dualistic Vedanta and an enlightened being who lived earlier in the 20th century. He was a math teacher before becoming a sannyasin, a renunciate or swami. His writings are collected in a set of volumes called "In the Woods of God Realization.

glowed and when he said to quit it was as if I heard it for the first time, but in a different way. Carole and I knew that we couldn't just *bring* this message into the documentary. We have to *be* the message." *Be the message* became their motto.

Once my friend Joanne typed the transcripts, Carole went over and over them. By the time she was finished highlighting what she would use, she knew them by heart. And she used this wisdom in her life every day, as did Alex. Soon, the four of us were reciting quotes to each other like:

"Choose Love, not fear."

"The consequences of not connecting to the Soul are pain and suffering."

"The thunderstorms are just as beautiful as a sunny day."

"The psyche is relentless. It wants to grow!"

"Trust really who you are!"

"Soul work is taking something painful.. and expressing it... in your creativity."

"Being creative gets me in touch with my spirituality... just digging in the garden!"

As Carole completed taking all this in she did two things. First, she announced that there was not just one documentary-- there were probably many more. She read off a list that I knew fit together. She said we had one on the spiritual nature of death and dying, healers and healing, near-death experiences, personal spirituality, healing from addictions, Soul work/creativity and more. The second thing was Carole became full of energy. As she worked in her head and heart to take in all the material and transform it into a coherent flow, she transformed her body.

She started by having a *truckload* of wood chips delivered (twice in one summer) and she single handedly spread them all over their yard. No matter how hot -- there she was sweating up a storm with a shovel in hand, making their property into a showplace. I would pull up and she would look at me and say, "Soul work is taking something painful and ... just digging in the garden!"

And as the rest of this story unfolded-- I watched her take her wounds from her childhood and go to deeper levels of their transformation and release.

CHAPTER 6

WHAT IS THE SOUL?

A few weeks later, there was a huge conference in Atlanta called 'The Whole Life Expo.' I gave a talk on Friday evening. Charlie spoke on Saturday afternoon, and then I drove him to the airport because he was speaking at a conference for survivors of child sexual abuse the next day in Providence, Rhode Island. I then went over to Carole and Alex's to spend the evening. They had been at Whole Life Expo too, but they were working for their documentary. They had their camera set up and were asking people walking by "What is the Soul?" The documentary was to begin with these 'man on the street' interviews.

The three of us were tired and lounging in the living room. Alex asked me if I had ever heard of a "didgeridoo" and I hadn't. He explained that it was a musical instrument of an indigenous tribe in Australia. They take a limb or root of a tree, usually a twisted one, and let termites hollow it out. Then it is painted and the mouth of it shaped for a musical instrument that is blown into. It takes practice to get sound out but it is worth it because the sound is beautiful and mystical. There was a booth at Whole Life Expo that was selling didgeridoos and he really wanted to buy one but decided not to spend the money on it just then.

It was almost December and I knew Alex had a birthday soon. "Alex, your birthday is coming up and I usually spend about $25. If I give it to you now, will that make the difference so you'll go and buy your didgeridoo?"

He thought for a moment and with a big smile said, "Yeah."

"Let's go." I said, getting my energy and enthusiasm back.

"You're kidding!" Carole laughed.

Alex and I both got up and we answered together, "No kidding. Let's go."

A half hour later, there we were-- walking among the booths: herbs, massage, jewelry, juices, books, tapes and CD's, and an array of psychics-- from card readers to mediums. Carole decided to have a reading and I wandered over to buy a little portable chair that was great for sitting on the floor at workshops. The chair booth was across the aisle from Alex who was getting some sound out of a didgeridoo. The woman in the booth said they are very hard to blow and Alex was doing great. I knew this was going to take some time so I went over and had a Polaroid picture taken of -- you guessed it-- my aura!

Then Carole was back and excited because the psychic told her that Diane Sawyer or Oprah Winfrey would be interested and involved in the documentary. Carole admired both women and I could tell she really wanted to believe it was true. The psychic even said that "This is much bigger than what you believe you have now. Steven Spielberg will get involved. There will be a book. You can't begin to imagine how this will turn out but it is much bigger than what you have now!"

Carole pulled me over to the psychic's booth so I could see her.

"Diane Sawyer," Carole kept repeating, and "Oprah Winfrey..."

"A book?" I asked as I watched Carole's face. She was lit up and talking as though she knew all this was going to happen, especially the part about Diane Sawyer. I had to say, "Carole, you are a real trip!"

What!" she said. "It could happen!"

Alex meanwhile had picked out a great didgeridoo and the sound he was getting was actually beautiful, almost supernatural. Alex's size and the strength of his lungs were already making an apparent difference because I was trying to blow in one and nothing happened.

Driving home all we talked about was Diane Sawyer. Carole knew she was the one who would introduce the documentary. I heard that many times over the next few months.

When we went back to the house, Carole took her Polaroid picture of her aura off the refrigerator and we compared. We had the identical aura. And so we kept saying, "See, I told you so!"

I always took it to mean that on some level we were kindred spirits.

SEEING THE INTERVIEWS

Alex and Carole had to translate their digitally recorded documentary interviews into VHS format. It took a month, and then we could watch them. I waited anxiously. The first one Carole and I watched together was the interview with David Nowe. David is a remarkable man, and I have always felt happy and lucky when I am with him. He's hard to explain. I was glad I took his workshop before the conference started. It takes a full day to understand and appreciate his work. And the richness and pureness of his intellect and spirituality certainly came across in his interview.

First, David said, "Soul essentially is the deepest part of our being. It's our Self. It's the Spirit within. When we experience a beautiful sunset, we often close our eyes because we feel so good and allow the sense of awe and the sense of joy to well up within. That sense of awe, that sense of beauty isn't in the sunset. It's within us. We recognize it."

Carole jumped and said, "That's it, number one sound bite for David." And she started writing. A few moments later David said, "That which we are looking for-- is that which is looking. And so we are looking for happiness. We're looking for God. We're looking for self- realization. We're looking. We're looking for something outside ourselves. But what we're really looking for is that which is looking, our own Self."

Toward the end of his interview he said, "True prayer is connecting to the Divine within-- becoming one with that. And as we connect with that divinity-- our bodies are healed, our minds are healed, our Souls are healed. We're brought into the recognition that we are already whole and perfect and complete as we are-- perfect children of God."

As David's interview finished, the joy and peace I had felt at the conference was back again. And now I had hope that it would be shared with an audience I couldn't even begin to imagine. I looked at Carole. She was flushed.

"Wow," I said.

She answered, "I know. I've watched it three times and I'm still blown away."

"Are the other's like this?"

"I've only watched a few. And each one has its unique impact. Here's Bonnie Greenwell's. I haven't seen hers. Let's watch it."

As her interview began, Bonnie was sitting by the Chattahoochee River and looked beautiful. The water behind her was reflecting sunlight in a serene way. Her hair caught the light, too. Her manner of speaking was relaxed and casual. Her comments were heartfelt, simply stated-- and I realized-- explained complex concepts in a way we could understand.

"The easiest way for us to think about it is that it is the life force. We all know we have energy in our body. When we die, this energy leaves the body. I know my little cat died. We had to have her put to sleep a few years ago. And I could hold her and I could feel the energy leaving her body. You can feel this. It's nothing that mysterious. The problem is that it isn't measurable, though, by medical science."

Later on, she said, "It's a wake up call-- to grow into who you really are. And let go of all the things that are blocking you from that experience. So, it's a good thing."

Alex and Carole had been careful to ask everyone they interviewed the question we hopefully wait to hear. 'Is there anything you would like to add? Take a few minutes.' Bonnie had tears dancing in her eyes when she gave her last answer. I watched her speak her most heartfelt hope for us, spirit and this planet. She ended with, "If we had a whole species of people that were allowed to feel wonderful and completely meet their own potential and never saw a barrier in any other human-- We could certainly have a different planet -- couldn't we?"

Carole and I looked at each other. We each took a deep breath. "If they're all like this-- our prayers have been answered," I said.

"Yeah." said Carole, looking puzzled or perhaps worried, "But if they're all like this-- I don't know how I can get through them. Every statement is so profound-- I keep getting lost in them. And I'm concerned about... I'm not sure. But it seems like we have big answers here. I don't know, maybe it's the darkness I remember from my childhood. What if someone else uses this great stuff for the wrong reasons?"

"Carole, Spirit is obviously coming through in these interviews. We're talking about how to heal, how to be whole, how to remember who we are-- innocent children of God. I'm pretty sure Spirit doesn't want us to stop here-- now. Maybe if you just think about surrendering to the process and just let Spirit work through you. I know your talent is important, or Spirit wouldn't choose to be working through you. Just remember that Spirit is doing this *with* you. Okay?"

She nodded, and said, "I have to jump in and have faith! This is about Spirit and we're trying to connect everyone to It."

We agreed we had watched enough and met again two days later. We watched my interview. There was a shift in the way I looked and sounded ten minutes into the tape when I began telling my NDE. I could see Spirit moving in-- like It did in the other interviews. Carole started writing when I gave the quote about *brand names*. I said, "I think where we are running into trouble as a global community now is in the idea that everybody is giving a different name to this energy. You know, I call it 'brand names.' In the Eastern Yogic tradition it is 'Kundalini.' Over here in the West, the Native Americans call it 'Great Spirit.' Christianity calls it 'Holy Spirit.' The Jewish people call it 'Ruach Ha Kadosh.' You know, God didn't put a brand name on It and tell us that one was right and one was wrong. This is generic!"

IN THE EDITING ROOM

Carole negotiated to edit at night because of some consideration on the cost. The first time we edited-- she confided in me as she drove the two of us there-- she felt like a kid who was taking her mother to school.

"That's okay," I told her. "In some ways I am like your mother, and I am definitely interested in your work. Furthermore, I know you've got talent and I want to watch it at work. So don't mind me. Just forget I'm with you. I'll sit back and be quiet." (That last line had me a little worried because I love to talk and usually have an opinion. I figured this might be the only time I would watch Carole edit. But that was all right too because I wanted a picture of her in my mind that I could cherish-- Carole painting her masterpiece. As spring turned into summer and the heat of summer wore on-- as long as I was in town-- I went to edit with Carole.)

The production company where we edited was beautiful and during the regular work day had a full kitchen with a chef who would come around with a cart at mealtimes to feed the clients and their crew. There was a long corridor with individual editing rooms flanking each side. Each room was decorated in impeccable taste. The room we were given when we arrived, and for the duration of the editing process, was large and well lit, with controls to dim the lights, too. Carole sat at a big desk in front of a wall of several TV screens and computer monitors. I sat to the side on a big lush leather sofa. Alex came in after work and sat at a table behind Carole. He got us to laugh occasionally because the work was so intense. He brought in dinner and we took a half hour to eat and chat. Then we watched what we had so far, and would go on-- sometimes until one or two in the morning.

We started each editing session with a prayer asking Spirit to help us to be 'Its instrument.' And, we asked Spirit to help 'us' get our egos out of the way so 'It' could come through in the documentary. In our first session, Carole fed each interview through the equipment and into the hard drive of the computer. She then started through the transcripts of each interview and found the sound bites she had highlighted on the printed transcripts. She watched the monitors as she ran the interview and found the sound bite. Then she marked it and did some other stuff that I didn't understand. I sunk back into the plush sofa and watched her work. I watched her back as her hands danced on the key board. I watched her immerse herself in the process, and as time went by-- I watched her genius- cut, copy and paste. I watched themes emerge. I watched Alex get her over some humps. I watched them debate whose ideas were calling each decision. I watched them laugh and then communicate in the cutest ways two people can communicate and debate. I saw them take turns winning. I felt more and more love for them.

Carole was working on a long quote from Jyoti who said, "I came out of an abusive marriage and was very unconscious in my way of relating and started to wake up. I started to see my wounds. And I started to see what my life was, and I wasn't pleased with where I had chosen to sit. That's the hardest part, when you wake up and you look around and you see. 'Why am I doing this?' 'What's this about?' 'Why am I letting people hurt me?' 'Why am I always allowing myself to always be the victim?' 'Is life about that?' I had been told it was: 'Just get by.' 'Just survive.' 'Don't make too much noise.' 'Don't say too much.'"

And later Jyoti said, "The thunderstorms are just as beautiful as a sunny day. And so is life. It's that same way. And so as people start to come through and break out of these old forms, it's really difficult because a lot of what they were told and they developed belief systems around-- has to crumble and fall down."

Carole's favorite quote of Jyoti's was, "Choose love not fear. It's a very simple thing. When you don't know what to do-- you just say, 'what would love do?' And make that choice."

The first time Carole put together a sequence of sound bites was a thrilling moment. David Nowe started with, "The consequences of not connecting to the Soul are pain and suffering-- pain and suffering--simply being disconnected from the source of our bliss. It's as simple as that."

Charlie said next, "We are stressed repeatedly and end up with stress-related disorders, diseases, emotional problems-- like arthritis, diabetes, allergies, cancer, accidents.

David comes back with, "The consequences of listening are joy, peace, abundance, ecstasy."

Then Lawrence says, "Because on a most profound level, being in touch with the wisdom of the Soul is being in touch with the power of love. When you stop to think about it, 'in love.' It's like-- love descends on us and we are in it. The power of love is a transpersonal power. It's not something you possess."

CHEMICAL DEPENDENCE, DISCONNECTION AND DESPAIR

Carole told us that the next theme that was emerging had to do with addictions because of our being disconnected from our own Souls and spirit. She started the program again and Lawrence Edwards said, "And so now what happens is we begin to then have to deal with the pain. And people begin to self-medicate themselves-- through alcohol, through drugs.'

Andrew Newberg, a young physician who is doing brain research said, "A lot of people who have different types of addictions-- have been known to have a negative view of God or look at God as being more punitive-- or a more negative emotional type of God.

At that point Carole slid in the beautiful quote from Jyoti saying, "You know, God's not scary. We are! Our mind makes up things that create fear."

Lawrence Edwards then said, "Our culture offers very few answers that have any depth to them. And what often happens is people go into a profound state of despair or resignation-- where you're meant to be essentially a combination of being a consumer and an achiever. Those answers don't satisfy our Soul. We can consume everything in sight from, you know, beautiful objects and jewelry to alcohol and drugs-- trying to be satisfied-- trying to quell that agitation that's going on in our spirit. And none of them touch it."

Alex asked, "Carole, we have a lot more quotes on addiction, don't we? We've got enough for another documentary just on that."

"Yes," she answered, "We have enough but we're just going to touch on it here-- enough that we are being realistic and grounded about all this. We're telling our audience briefly about the pain of being disconnected from our Souls and then we're going to show them how to directly connect. We're probably going to have two strong segments on spiritual practice, especially prayer and meditation. Here, watch this..."

Lawrence Edwards started again and said, "Meditation so hones the mind, so strengthens the power of the mind that you can take on and do that thing you didn't think you could do before. And what I began to find in the practice of meditation was that truthfully-- 'Oh! You get high doing this.' You start having experiences that weren't available even through drugs. And not only that, I didn't feel bad at the end. I didn't feel bad physically, I didn't feel bad emotionally, I didn't feel guilty about it. I couldn't get arrested for it. There seems to be no down side to this. So I began practicing meditation on a regular basis-- every day."

Then Charlie said, "I find spirituality in my life in a number of ways. One of them is through meditation. I also use prayer. I read spiritual literature and share some of that with others. And then other ways is working with plants, just digging in the garden. Being creative, I think, gets me in touch with my spirituality."

And then we watched David Nowe teaching us to meditate.

It was all coming together.

CHAPTER 7

MILLENNIUM BABY

Carole completed the medication she had been on for a year. She had lost three or four nails but her skin remained free of acne. The time had finally come for her to be able to have dermabrasion. Before she did it, I went with her to a plastic surgeon who told us about the alternative to dermabrasion. The surgeon would actually cut out two or three deep scars and use a laser on the rest. It sounded much more traumatic. Carole and Alex were also beginning to talk about having a baby, so she opted for the dermabrasion.

It was done on a Friday morning as an out-patient. Alex went with her. They called when they came home and asked me to come over. Carole had several bandages of assorted sizes and shapes. They didn't need changing for 24 hours and we decided I would come over the next day and we three would change them together.

The next afternoon, the three of us sat in the living room with tension mounting. We talked for an hour and a half about any and everything; the documentary, Diane Sawyer, the didgeridoo, getting pregnant, why their dog and three cats were acting weird, etc. Finally, because I knew I had things to do at home, I suggested we change the bandages. We looked at each other with the tension hovering. We decided to do it in the bathroom.

We walked Carole in and she stood in front of the mirror. There were seven different shaped bandages on her face. Each one needed to be soaked off with a prescribed liquid and replaced by a clean bandage of approximately the same shape-- after it was coated with an ointment. Carole put some liquid on a cotton ball and tried to moisten the top of one bandage. She gave it a little tug and jumped. She started walking quickly around the room and telling us how bad this was. She began catastrophizing. I didn't know what to do-- or what would happen next.

Alex gently placed both hands on Carole's shoulders and guided her to their bed where he told her to lie down. She protested. She had to see in the mirror. I grabbed a small round mirror off the counter and gave it to her. She held the mirror over her face and continued talking rapidly about how awful this all was. I quickly soaked cotton balls and handed them to her-- grabbing the one she had just used. She soaked a bandage with the cotton ball while Alex cut a new bandage-- trying to duplicate the same shape. At the same time he was cutting, he was joking and interrupting her with teasing and singing.

The first bandage came off and all we saw was reddish pink skin. "Oh! That's not so bad." Carole said. Alex started singing, "That's not so bad" in his deep bass voice. We went to the next bandage, and then the next. I was so nervous that occasionally I would lose my rhythm and either drop a cotton ball or have to throw away a new bandage I had just put ointment on.

It took us about 20 minutes and then we were back in the living room talking about how that wasn't so bad!

On Sunday afternoon we started earlier. Alex sang and I soaked cotton balls and coated bandages with ointment. Carole was flat on her back in bed looking in the mirror and peeling off bandages. Her face was redder and we could see where some of the scars were shallower and others were almost gone. Alex was funnier and we were relieved. We now saw what we were dealing with.

Alex was really funny with his wise-cracks and singing in between. I looked at these two in this hilarious scene and started laughing. Carole was being a perfectly neurotic Carole and Alex was coaxing her through in such a delightful, intelligent and tender way. I fell into the bed next to Carole, holding my sides because of the laughter spilling out of me.(And I knew in my heart I wasn't just laughing at us-- but adoring both of them.)

Alex started laughing, too. Carole started to get angry and then caught our laughter. We were hilarious. We howled for several minutes. After that, the tension disappeared. We had stopped 'the changing of the bandages' (as we called it with a great deal of respect!) and finally breathed into our laughter.

When we finished, I told them they didn't need me anymore. They could do 'the changing of the bandages' for the next week themselves until they went back to the doctor.

GETTING READY FOR A BABY

The documentary's contents were coming together. Carole, Alex and I went over the video in their living room and talked about it. Then we went back to the editing studio and she made a few more changes. Basically, we were thrilled. The message was so rich, so real-- so connected spiritually. We were not only delighted-- we were full of gratitude. And Carole said, "Now this baby is born! And, we can get ready for our next baby!"

Carole made an appointment to see an obstetrician to get ready for her biological baby. The doctor told her she should not be alarmed by the tests she had taken in the past which pointed to pre-cancerous findings. This doctor told her she should go ahead and have her baby. She even said that other patients who had a history of childhood sexual abuse have unexplainable test findings. They would closely monitor Carole but she also needed to get on with her life.

First I heard all the reasons why Alex and Carole weren't ready and then all the reasons they were just about ready. I love babies and I sensed that I had another grandbaby coming soon. I got excited.

Carole was doing yoga, getting massages, doing everything she could do to get ready to be the mother she wanted to be. She was determined not to pass her pain on to her child, as she now knew was often the case. Carole saw the birth of the baby as a second chance, an opportunity to change the future by healing from the past. I told them when they did have their baby I would baby-sit at least once a week so they could go out alone together. Of course, I considered this to be a selfish act because I really wanted this baby all to myself.

RENEWAL OF VOWS

Carole and Alex drove up to Cashiers, North Carolina for the long Easter weekend. She told me, "We wanted to go to this wonderful place called The Innisfree Inn to make our first baby-- a millennium baby hopefully. Alex kept saying, 'The Innisfree Inn is not free but it sure is worth it!'

Carole described the details of the trip, saying:

"The drive was beautiful. First we went to the Atlanta Diner for a nice brunch. I had the Lumberjack-- I ate more food than Alex--huge pancakes, some ham, bacon and sausages, eggs too. You get the picture?

"Anyhow, it was an unseasonably warm day--around the low 80's, sunny and clear. Once we were in the mountains it got a little scary with all the twists and curves, not to mention all the crazy drivers who like to drive around bends in your lane instead of theirs. These mountains which sit at the tip of the Great Smokies have been said to be the oldest in the world and they sit right on the Eastern Continental Divide. There are mountain laurel and rhododendron everywhere sticking straight up out of granite rock. Arriving there was magical, like entering a dream.

"We got to the Inn at five o'clock. Driving up the steep driveway and seeing the expanse of land with the little blue carriage house on the right brought sudden waves of deja-vu from the trip we had taken together to New Hope, Pennsylvania when we first met. I remember at the time we had ventured onto this beautiful farm property and parked right outside of a little house that looked just like this one and I felt that I should be staying there for some reason. It was as if I had previously seen into the future."

"Oh Carole, I've had those too. I call them 'future memories.'

"Yeah, that's what they are. The next day, Easter, Alex and I climbed the mountain we were told about. It took us several hours and it was a hard climb. It is suppose to be a powerful energy vortex (a place where peace is concentrated and emanates through veins of energy coming from the planet). The climb was hard but I was glad we did it. When we got to the top the view was spectacular. And then Alex and I pulled out the Renewal of Vows we had written to each other and we stood facing each other on the top of this mountain and read our Vows to each other. Would you like to see what we wrote? I want to share it with you, Barbara."

Teary- eyed, I took the papers from her and read hers first.

RENEWAL OF VOWS

April 4, 1999

On this very special Easter day, the last of the 20th century,
I, Carole, again take you Alex
as my husband in this lifetime and as my Soul mate in eternal time.
God and the Divine Mother are our witness on this vortex of Peace.
You are the light of my life,
The food of my Soul.
I love you from the depth of my being.
Now, Always and Forever.
I am so connected to you.
You are like the air I breathe.
You are cherished.
You are divine.
I promise to be the best friend I can to you,
to appreciate you for the wonderful, unique individual that you are
and to put your well-being before my own needs.
I promise to stand with you always at your side,
to be your partner.
a source of strength and understanding.
I vow to live life with you,
to really live and enjoy without fear.
I promise to share with you my True Self,
To co-create joy and peace.
And surrender to you
All that I am.
God bless us and our holy union.

Then she handed me Alex's.

To Carole--- A Vow of Love
by Alex

Seven years have come and gone...
Good times, bad times, that made us strong.
I now reflect upon our eternal vow...
To love and cherish forever more.
I'm comforted as I ponder how...
Our love is stronger then before.
Friends, and lovers and Soul mates are we...
Our roots grow strong from our mighty tree.
And now we pray to bear our fruit...
The child who begins our dynasty.
I look to God and reconfirm...
The love inside my heart that burns.
I pledge to always keep you by my side...
Our true love I will first abide.
You alone will be my wife...
This I vow for all my life.
To honor, respect and understand...
My heart is in your command.
So when the days of future pass...
You may question if our love will last.
Always remember our eternal vow...
To love each other right here and now.

DIANE SAWYER AND GOOD MORNING AMERICA

Carole and I were meeting for coffee. I watched her stroll in and give her order. She almost skipped over to me--cup in hand, dancing eyes and a huge grin.

"What's up?" I asked.

Carole answered, almost singing, "Remember I told you a few weeks or so ago that I heard Good Morning America with **Diane Sawyer** !! wanted to know if any couples were planning to have a millennium baby. Well, they are bringing two couples to New York to be on TV with **Diane Sawyer**!!"

"Yeah," I laughed. "So?"

"We're going! We're going!" she was laughing and jumping.

"I don't believe it! Wow! From now on anything you focus on-- I will believe. You are amazing. You wanted Diane Sawyer for the documentary and now they are flying you to New York to be on Good Morning America with Diane Sawyer!"

"Yeah, Well --there's that little catch. It might be just a little embarrassing talking about how we're going to get pregnant that night! But Alex and I have agreed we'll get through it! I can't wait to meet her. I *love* Diane Sawyer!!" Carole was singing her words again.

I sat there shaking my head... "You are a powerful woman! What you set your mind to-- you get. You are amazing.... You are a 'power to be reckoned with!' So what are you going to wear?"

"I don't know... Maybe that striped jersey and the black pants I bought last week with you. Remember?" Carole said. We both had tears in our eyes.

They flew to New York on Thursday.

Charlie and I and everyone we know were up early the next morning to watch. And there they were on the screen with the other couple that was brought in. Diane Sawyer sat facing them.

She said, "Joining us now are two couples who hope to ring in the new year with a newborn." She introduced the first couple and then said, "And this is Alex and Carole from Atlanta, Georgia. They've been married for five years. What are you doing here? (laughing) What are you doing here talking about this? (laughing.) Alex, Carole how did you decide to do this? Why now?"

Carole answered, "Well, at first we were trying to avoid Y2K from all the reports and the scare of meltdown and all that."

Diane Sawyer: Right. About being in the hospital when the computers collapse and all that?

Carole: Right. I sort of wanted to avoid the situation. But it's something we've been thinking about -- having children -- for a while and it sort of came to the time and we're ready. We've done a lot of things to get ready for a baby. And we just decided it would be fun to have a baby.

Diane Sawyer: So what sort of things are you doing. (Laughs) Well, I know what sort of things you're doing. But I mean what *sort* of things are you doing?

Alex: Well, on a responsibility note we quit smoking and we're doing all these things to try to be great parents. You know, the time is coming and we're getting all this advice like keep your legs in the air for ten minutes and all these different crazy things. And I'm saying 'What are you talking about?'"

Diane Sawyer (looking at Alex): You're suppose to keep your legs...

Alex: No. No. It's not me... (Laughter)

Diane Sawyer: Just checking to see how much you researched it. (Laughing and turning her attention to the other couple for several questions.) Then she again looked toward Carole and Alex and asked:

"Alex, when you go to the office what do people say to you?"

"Well, Carole and I had a conversation about ten days ago that we were going to keep this a secret. We forgot we wrote you a note. (laughter) So upon knowing that we were going on Good Morning America-- we had to let people know because as someone astute pointed out 'you're going to be on national news.' So we definitely all of a sudden got a lot of ribbing-- excuse me-- I did. People were calling and saying things like 'go get um tiger. Way to go, stud!' One guy called me 'Alex G Spot' (they all laugh) So, it's been a peculiar situation to say the least. (laughter)

Diane Sawyer: Well, count on us to keep your secrets. Right? (laughter) You're just among friends here... All of us! (more giggles) So when will you know?

All four: In a few weeks.

Diane Sawyer: In a few weeks and you'll be sure to contact us. Right?

All four: Yeah! in a few weeks.

Diane Sawyer: All right. And we'll accompany you.(laughter) In the days ahead. Again, it's great to see you. I have to tell you, I got a briefing note about all of you and at the bottom it says 'they are so cute and have great personalities!' I think the briefing note was right and good luck to all of you and I think you're mad! Completely crazy! We'll be back in a moment...

Charlie and I sat quietly for a few minutes taking it all in. We talked about how cute they looked. And then we talked about the thrill of having a new Soul coming into our lives. My heart was so filled. I thought of all the times Carole and I would take the baby and go where mothers and daughters go when they are together with a baby-- the park, the mall, just a walk around the block.

We had dinner at their house the night they came back. They told us that they didn't ask Diane Sawyer directly about her viewing the documentary because they were so taken by her. They talked at great length about her radiance and her beauty. They did however, talk to the producer who was willing to listen and said to send it along when it was ready and they would view it. Carole repeated the words she wrote in the note that got them on the show. It was referring to the Y2K fears, so they wrote: "We've decided to choose **love** not **fear**. What better way is there to start a new millennium than to bring life into the world with love?"

SUCCESS AND COMPLICATIONS

I was in Sarasota staying with my daughter, Beth. She had been sick for a while and needed me while her husband Ed flew to New England for his father's emergency surgery. I had been there about a week when Carole called. Actually, she had called several times to see how Beth was doing But this time was different. We had a long talk. I coaxed her to tell me what was going on. She hesitated because of Beth's being sick. She was sensitive to our situation, but as I continued coaxing her, she said that she had taken a pregnancy test that morning and that it was positive. I was so excited. I reassured her and told her that it was wonderful to hear her good news. Beth was excited too. We talked about how she and Alex hadn't made the millennium conception date-- but 'who cares.' They were having a baby and that's all we could talk about.

I drove home from Beth and Ed's a few days later and when I arrived in Atlanta I called Carole. We made arrangements for the four of us to get together that evening and celebrate.

A few weeks later I went back to Sarasota because Beth needed surgery. Carole called me upset. She had bled the night before and was checked by a physician in the obstetric practice that I had suggested she go to. Her blood levels were low for the pregnancy. They should be doubling every 24 hours-- so she would go back for more blood work the next day.

A few days later I went with Carole for another check up. We saw the ultrasound that showed the fetus in the sack. There was no heart beat. Her numbers on the pregnancy hormone blood test were climbing, but *slowly*, in no way doubling like they should be. The ultrasound technician told us there should be a heart beat visible by now. Next, the doctor came in and talked about doing a D&C. Carole said she wasn't ready to have one yet. The doctor told her to wait a few more days and come back, which she did. The next ultrasound showed the sack and where the fetus had appeared a few days earlier was now a mass that didn't look as formed. They told us it was "breaking down."

We saw a different physician every time, but each one was compassionate--One even told us about her own loss of an early pregnancy and her subsequent D&C. She had tears in her eyes as she told Carole several times during the conversation that she understood her disappointment, pain and sadness. Both times I went with Carole-- Alex met us there from work.

Carole and Alex wanted to wait another week. They wanted to give this baby every chance before taking it away. They even got a second opinion. That doctor confirmed what the others were saying.

A week later they went in for an outpatient D&C. The night before she went in, she called me and expressed the need for some kind of a ceremony afterwards to help with her sadness and the baby's Soul journey to complete itself. I told her I'd be over tomorrow, late afternoon and we would do some kind of spontaneous ritual. She and Alex could think about what they wanted to do and I would follow along.

I noticed a week earlier that I had a pain in my lower left side. I asked Carole what her pain felt like and as she described it --realized I was carrying some of Carole's pain, more diffuse, but it was there. I told Carole about that and she added that she was relieved that this pregnancy wasn't an ectopic one. She said she had been afraid of that. She spoke many times of her fear of an ectopic pregnancy. After Carole's D & C, the pain in my side didn't go away.

"Everything that can go wrong with me physically always has. It seems that everywhere my father touched me needs to be scraped. After the D&C my uterus will be clean and then maybe I can have a healthy pregnancy with a healthy baby. But my body always does the worst stuff. Look at my face. My skin was good until I got my memories back of the abuse."

"Carole, your face is not ruined. You are beautiful. You always have been and you always will be." I said.

She blushed "Yeah, in your eyes."

"The dermabrasion really has helped. Your skin's not perfect. But we humans aren't perfect. Remember what Charlie and his colleagues say, 'The body keeps the score!'"

"Yeah, well mine sure has. I have skin like my father's and everywhere he's abusively touched my body-- I have problems." Carole said. "I'm just relieved that this pregnancy made it into my uterus and not in my tube!"

CHAPTER 8

UNCONDITIONAL PRESENCE

Carole called as soon as she and Alex came home from the hospital. I waited a few hours so she could nap, then went over. She was in the living room on the sofa with her feet up, and a blanket of suns, moons and stars covering her knees. I sat next to her and in her big bright-eyed way, she announced to me that she was totally in the moment. "Just like you wrote about in *Final Passage*. I'm in 'unconditional presence.' I know this is grieving, but it's just like you wrote-- still an amazing state of consciousness."

Carole spoke of how this book was teaching her how to grieve. She ended with "My heart is wide open from the grieving. The sadness keeps it open. Oh! I know I'll get through this--- I hate the pain but the state I'm in is also amazing because I feel riveted in the moment!! You do understand-- don't you Barbara?"

"I do, Carole. I do. I'm just so sorry, that you have to go through this."

Her pixie face scrunched up into a painful look. "Just a few weeks ago we were on top of the world. Alex loved his job and we were having a baby. Now, Alex hates his job and the baby is gone."

"The pregnancy is gone, Carole. But the baby's Soul is still here. I can sort of see, no feel a presence up to your left, my right. It is probably waiting to come back in another pregnancy. This Soul's not leaving." I answered.

"Yea, that's what that fellow said the other night over at the dinner party. He had psychic abilities and could see a Soul up above me on the same side you are saying."

She looked tired and wrung out. I felt that way too.

I swept some of her hair from her cheek and said softly, "I love you Carole…. We're going to get through this. Give yourself some time to heal. And grieve for as long as you need. Just remember I love you and I'm always here for you."

"Yea." she said with that look that made her whole face twinkle, "Well maybe we can both be here for Shannon. Did I tell you what she did?"

I looked over in the corner of the dining room and there glued to the floor with her chin on her front paws was the cocker spaniel. Only her eyes would move.

"The dog is so funny. She's my shadow. She feels everything I feel. I came home so down and she started running around doing her thing that usually makes me laugh. You know, front paws and chin down on the floor with her rump and tail straight up in the air going 90 miles an hour. Then she barked and pranced. You know, her whole routine. She kept it up for 15 or 20 minutes and then realized I wasn't going to cheer up so she went into a complete funk and now look at her. She's been in that corner for hours." Only her eyes moved as we talked about the sight of her looking so depressed made us both laugh.

Alex came in and grinned at the dog, too. Then he reminded us that we had planned to go in the yard, build a fire and have a ceremony for the loss of the baby. He added that he needed the ceremony, too.

We walked out to the back yard and I sat on one of the two park benches while Alex moved in and out of the house bringing out his didgeridoo and Carole's drum. Carole crouched next to the fire pit and arranged twigs and branches that had dropped from the stately oaks surrounding us. In the darkness of night only the stars and a quarter moon lit the scene as I watched Carole's silhouette prepare the fire as women have done for thousands and thousands of years. She blew gently into the smoke. Her profile was that of a beautiful young girl as she re-arranged twigs. She reminded me of a young Goddess-- perhaps Hestia the archetype for the bringer of fire to each hearth.

"Carole," I asked, "Have you heard of the Goddess Hestia? When the people would move in to a new house or hut-- she would come and light the hearth for the first time. She was the bringer of fire. I'm watching you and..."

As she glanced at me with the moon light on her face, I could no longer speak. There was a jolt inside of me-- of a memory of something beyond here.

"I know," she said in almost a whisper. "Me, too. I love this."

"Were we together?" my voice was almost a whisper and raspy.

"Of course!" she answered with a hint of a giggle. "*We've* been together before."

I said, "I know. I know." barely audible even to myself, as we glanced at each other and the new fire exposed our faces. Our brief eye contact with the fire's orange glow revealing us-- acknowledged some kind of spiritual significance that felt like a time warp.

That moment transcended this lifetime. I have relived this memory over and over in my mind and my heart. It -- we-- felt out of time... and connected to each other in that eternal infinite place where we had known each other for eons. The fire crackled as our hearts acknowledged a deep union with each other and all of creation.

A few moments later, Alex, sitting with Carole on the other bench, was blowing his didgeridoo melodically. Carole was beating her drum and we speculated that the neighbors had to think we were crazy. With that bit of humor in the background we each said a prayer for the baby's Soul.

Carole expressed gratitude for her miscarriage's being quick and over. She blessed the baby's Soul and asked it to have patience. She asked that she would become pregnant again easily. She asked for her and Alex's healing over all this, and if the baby's Soul needed healing, that the Soul would receive healing too.

And then, Alex asked for Carole's healing and his. He asked that the baby's Soul feel their love and 'hang in there.' Then Alex got up and moved in front of me. He was silent for a moment and then thanked me for my deep caring for them. My heart skipped a beat with surprise and then was wide open to him-- to them-- they were my dear friends, Soul family, my God children. The fire was blazing as Alex honored me with his words and I thought—"It's so natural to care for them. I love them with all my heart." And then it was my turn to speak. I thanked God for the blessing of Alex and Carole's friendship and love. And I told the baby's Soul that I was waiting to love it as soon as it could come back, which I prayed would be soon.

Then, we prayed together for Carole's strength to return and for both of them to heal from their loss. I thanked them for their love and we all thanked the Universe for each other...

The fire was down to a few glowing embers. I kissed them both and got in my car and drove home.

PRAYERS AND BUTTERFLIES

Carole decided she had been in the house long enough. Actually, when she called me she said she had 'cabin fever.' We laughed and agreed to meet for coffee in an hour.

Carole said, "I keep *Final Passage* on my bedside table and have been reading it off and on since the D&C. I read your story again about your mother. I guess I've been thinking a lot about mothers lately-- and about being a mother.

"Barbara, you sound like you have love for your mother yet I know how she abused you. I don't understand how you can...how can that be? I mean, I've thought... I've had so much time to think... How could my mother let my father abuse my sister and me the way he did?"

I looked deeply into her clear blue eyes. I knew I could say anything to her. I thought about even if she didn't-- or I couldn't help her to understand-- she wouldn't judge what I was saying. "I can remember when I was a little girl. I can remember looking at my mother when she was busy doing something else and I could see her as a little girl-- or maybe it is her Soul that I am seeing-- But I can -- or could-- see her behind the abuse that was done to her. I could see her as an innocent child of God before all the layers of wounding and scars that became my mother. She has a beautiful Soul. I know it."

Carole was quiet for a while. Her eyes wandered out the window and I sipped my coffee and thought about my mother. Finally, Carole turned her attention back to me and with tears in her eyes said, "I've always loved my mother... And my dad. It's hard to feel it and yet when I try I can. I can put their wounding and what they did to me aside for a split second and remember their goodness. They have it too. I'm sure they were wounded just like I was. And behind their wounding they have Souls that are yearning to be set free again. What can we do? How can we help them? We can pray for them -- Can't we?"

I nodded yes.

"I'll pray for them." she continued. Then she looked at her hands, inflamed from her eczema and she smiled. "And, I'll pray hard for myself, compassion for me and compassion for them."

We were quiet for a very long time. Finally, Carole pulled her copy of *Final Passage* out of her purse. She opened it to the epilogue and with tears occasionally falling down her cheeks she read my words so sweetly that she moved me to tears too:

Someone told me a story about a man who had been watching a butterfly struggling to get out of its cocoon. The man watched a while and then became concerned for the butterfly because it didn't seem to be freeing itself. He got a handsaw and sawed down the limb to which the cocoon was attached. Then he brought the cocoon into the house, took a small pair of scissors and carefully opened it to help the butterfly free itself more easily. The butterfly freed itself and rested, then fluttered some more. Finally, it stopped. It had died. Upset over what he had just witnessed, the man started doing research on the life of a butterfly. What he learned was that the butterfly needs to struggle for a long time to get out of its cocoon. In the struggle, hormones are produced that strengthen the wings for flight. Without the long struggle, the butterfly's wings will never become strong enough to support it, and it will soon die.

So too, our lives can be full of struggle. But without the struggle, perhaps we couldn't survive, learn to fully live and grow

to our potential. Our struggle in life is to move toward selfhood --
to become all that we are. Selfhood is our butterfly state.

She closed the book and our eyes met again. We didn't try
to talk...

Finally, Carole broke the silence with, "I love that story of
the butterfly. It makes my struggle--it makes everyone's struggle -
- all right. I'm going to edit in butterflies to the documentary for
transitions -- symbolizing transformation-- and I want to add you
telling this story because it gives all of our struggles in life
meaning.

S'MORE

It was Saturday and we decided to have a light dinner
together and then build a fire and make S'mores. So the four of us
shared a quiche and salad and waited for it to get dark enough for
the fire.

Carole was reflecting on the closure she was seeing on the
battle against the 'falsies.' She said the falsies were finally losing
the 'memory wars.' Charlie had an important paper being
published with two other authors in *The Journal of Psychiatry and
Law*. He was also asked to be a member of what was being called
'the Leadership Council.' and he had just been offered a consulting
position at the Centers for Disease Control and Prevention.

She asked Charlie about the paper and he told her the
Psychiatry and Law article was an extensive review of the state of
the art and science of the recovered memory dispute. The journal
is read mainly by lawyers, judges and their clerks.

Carole asked, "What exactly will a judge know after reading
it?"

"Judges will know that the science of traumatic memory and dissociative amnesia is now thoroughly proven by 68 studies, most of which are peer reviewed. Dissociative/traumatic amnesia is a documented part of the natural history of the effects of the trauma of child sexual abuse and other traumas as well. And finally juxtaposing the science with the law, it is inappropriate and unfair to allow 'false' memory testimony into the courts without allowing expert witnesses to testify about 'repressed memory'-- which the courts commonly refer to, and as what we call dissociative or traumatic amnesia.

"And what about the Leadership Council? What is it?"

"It's a group of clinicians and scientists-- mostly physicians -- psychiatrists whose goal is to bring accuracy to the media and in publications about mental health issues.

"This is great! And Barbara says you have been offered a position at the CDC?"

"Yes, I'm consulting on projects and publications that are related to the effects of child trauma, abuse and neglect on adult health and functioning. This is in part related to a large and important study about the long term effects of childhood trauma, which can also be called 'adverse childhood experiences' or 'ACEs' for short. The people I will be working with are pioneers in the epidemiology of medical and psychological problems among survivors of childhood trauma. They are making a large and important contribution to this mostly neglected aspect of medicine and psychology. Their research of a large population is proving what we have known for awhile. There is a strong relationship between the amount of exposure to abuse or household dysfunction during childhood and risk factors for several of the leading causes of death in adults. In other words, the body keeps the score. As health care providers we keep helping or aiding our patients' complaints or diseases that have surfaced. But we're not going to the root of the problem. We need to go deeper into our patients' histories and find out if past trauma isn't the real culprit."

"Boy, that's so great! It's happened. We can relax." Carole said as she sunk back in her chair.

"Oh, no we can't!" I smiled. "We've got a fire to prepare and s'mores to make."

LAST TIME TOGETHER

I took my mini-van over to the dealership for service. Carole picked me up while they were working on it and we went for lunch. She had seen a healer the day before because her eczema was continuing not only to bother her, but to bleed. Alex and she joked that her hands and feet were bleeding as though they were the stigmata.

She told me that the healer had talked her through a guided imagery that Carole was quite hopeful about. "I feel like I released the anger I had with my parents, especially my mother. I know this doesn't let them off the hook. They still have a lot of work to do on themselves, but I feel like I released the heaviness I was carrying. Maybe now my hands and feet can heal. If only I could take the medication for it. But I don't dare. Not if I'm going to try to get pregnant again. Oh! And I was told about this great herb that is made into an ointment for eczema. I ordered it from Australia over the Internet."

I asked her to tell me about the guided imagery.

"She had me visualize each of my parents with a ball in their hands. My father's ball was green and contained my healing.

My mother ball was blue and contained my peace. I asked them both to throw me the balls because they belonged to me. My father threw me the ball filled with my healing and my mother hesitated and I asked her again. Finally, she threw me the ball filled with my peace... And then I had to throw them each a ball that I could give them. I threw my father a ball filled with truth and I threw my mother a beautiful purple ball that was filled with spirituality. The healer gave me the visual but the actual colors and meaning of each ball just appeared in my awareness. I was choked up and I know--I can feel that this was profound."

"Oh Carole," I was feeling the fullness of her emotion now. "That's wonderful."

"Yeah, I know. It's my part completed but they still have theirs. You know, my mother stopped our family from healing when she went to that 'falsie' scientific board member. She let that woman convince her that my sister and I had the false memories. She *must* know deep in her heart that that's not true. My father had already written us the letter confessing for sexually abusing us, and apologizing. So, I sent him truth, and I pray he will find truth again. And if my mother can connect with her own natural spiritual self, maybe she can make this turn around, because she has bought in to the whole wrongness of all this by making my father retract his admission and apology, and reverse his stand and that forced us away. If she has Spirit helping her, I know she can reverse what she has created." Carole finished in a low voice because she was choking up and losing her voice.

"I hope, no... I'll pray for your parents, Carole. And, honey, I want you to know that I feel all of my prayers (and then I remembered the prayers we had done together before each healing session on her hands and feet) No, I'll change that to all of *our* prayers have been answered... You really have released...

You've unhooked yourself from this terrible situation -- haven't you?"

"Yeah," she answered, "I've let go of my part of my sister's and my own painful abuse from our childhood, and the way our parents treated us just a few years ago when we tried to heal this family. I've thrown the ball into their court now. Now, it's their turn. They won't feel a tug coming from me anymore. I've let go. They need to embrace the truth now, what really happened, and then maybe they can forgive themselves.

We were quiet for a long time.

"I'm glad you and Alex are going away for a long weekend. You both need to rest and hold hands and walk on the beach. And you can get your hands and feet back in the ocean."

Carole smiled and said, "Yeah! It hurts like hell when I put my hands and feet in the salt water. But then all the pain goes away. Alex gets a real kick out of me. I go running into the water -- and I'm yelping with all the stinging-- then I go 'Aaaahhhh!' when the pain is gone."

Her smile turned into a laugh as she described herself running into the ocean.

"I know, I know. Sometimes things hurt *good*!" I said noticing that special twinkle in her eyes. I smiled back, but in my heart I knew her pain remembering all the times I had held her hands and feet. Then I looked into her eyes again and realized that the twinkle was part of a light hearted giggle that was erupting from very deep inside of her. I thought again of the guided imagery she had just described and realized she had come full circle in her healing. I could feel it in her laughter...

"Are you going to that same place you've gone before?" I asked.

"No. I don't want to know where we are going to wind up. I want to wander on down to Florida without a plan. We seem to get better places -- better rooms and everything when we don't plan. We just meander and let Spirit lead us."

And she drove me back to the dealership. I remember waving as she pulled off with the straw hat I had given her on the back window. The last thing I said to her through the car window as she pulled off was, "Wear your hat, Carole. Don't let the sun on that pretty face."

I will always remember the love on her face as she drove away. Carole blew me a kiss and smiled.

CHAPTER 9

THE TERRIBLE NEWS

Charlie and I had just returned from a matinee. We saw *Sixth Sense* with Bruce Willis and this amazing young boy who deserves an academy award for his performance. He portrayed a child who could see ghosts. The ghosts turn out to be Souls who didn't know they were dead or couldn't leave because they need to complete something. The film was done amazingly well.

As soon as we came home, I called my daughter Beth. She had an appointment that day with the surgeon who had operated on her a few months earlier. I was still exhausted from watching her suffer through that surgery and bracing myself for two more operations she needed in the near future. She wasn't home. I left a message on her tape.

Next, I called Carole to see if they had returned home yet from their weekend getaway. I chuckled to myself as I realized they would now find three messages from me over the four days they were gone. The first message was to tell them that we were going to meet Bill Moyers next month. I asked them on their tape if that would be a good contact for the documentary. The second message was telling Carole I had gotten back my copy of *The Sai Prophecy,* a book I was sure she wanted to read because they were starting their plans to go to India to see the Avatar Sai Baba. And this new message was just, "Oh, you're not home yet. Give me a call when you settle in."

I still couldn't believe we met her and Alex only three years ago. It had been a fast and huge connection that covered mostly -- no *every* aspect of who we four are. I smiled as I thought of

Charlie's answering the phone whenever Carole called. He always said, "Barbara, it's your *other* daughter."

The phone rang. As I answered it I heard my son Gary tell me that Carole was in an ICU unit in Florida where they had been vacationing. She had collapsed and was in a coma. He told me everything he knew and I felt my knees turn to Jell-O. I went numb. I was sobbing, but as though from a distance. We talked for a few moments about how I could reach Alex and then we hung up. The evening is a blur now. Carole was somewhere near Ft. Walton Beach in the panhandle of Florida. I paged Alex at the hospital over and over and finally got Carole's sister, who was already there with her parents. I couldn't believe it. How did they get there so soon? Carole hadn't talked to her parents in seven years. What would she think or feel when she opened her eyes and saw them there? Where was Alex?

Charlie called the intensive care unit directly and within a matter of moments a neurologist called back and explained Carole's condition to him. He told Charlie that her pupils were fixed and dilated. We both knew that was a bad sign.

My heart and my mind were all over the place until Alex finally called around midnight. He said her condition was grave and asked me to come. "She needs to feel your energy Barbara. And she needs to hear your voice."

"Alex, I'll take the first flight out in the morning. I'll try to get there before noon. Where do I go?"

"Land in Ft. Walton Beach and then take a cab. It's only a few minutes to the Niceville Hospital. Yeah, I said 'Niceville' and everyone is. This whole thing is surreal."

"Alex," I asked before we hung up. How did Carole's parents get there?"

I heard him sigh deeply and explain, "I called her sister and then they called me. They asked if they could come. I know Carole would want it this way. They have unfinished business and I had to let them come. The one thing though is I told them they can't go in to see her alone. They must wait for me to take them in."

I was grateful Alex had put that one limit on them. When Carole woke up it would be shocking for her if they were standing there looking at her. She would need to be prepared, and Alex's being with them would make it all right.

I arranged a 10:15 a.m. flight and then never slept. I tossed and turned, talking to Carole. I had to believe she would come out of the coma. This was so unfair. She had so much to live for. I also couldn't believe the details of her condition. I went through their miscarriage with them only a month earlier. The doctors told her to wait for two menstrual cycles before trying to get pregnant again. I had seen two ultrasounds and the baby was not alive. There was no heart beating. And now Alex tells me that she had been pregnant and it was a tubal pregnancy that ruptured, and that she bled internally so fast that there was no blood to oxygenate and nourish her brain. The CPR that Alex and the EMTs attempted was not successful.

I tossed some more and thought of how Carole always said that anything she went through of a physical nature always had complications. "That seems to be typical." Charlie and I told her, "children of trauma especially those who suffered physical or sexual abuse tend to have more chronic illnesses and may get more complications." These words kept echoing in my head. I never slept. Those quotes kept playing over and over.

Occasionally, I would tear myself away from all my fears and think instead of the movie we had just seen-- *Sixth Sense.* It brought me no comfort at all.

I left early for the airport and sat at the gate for over an hour. I talked to Carole, silently in my mind. "Don't leave, Honey. Please stay. I love you. Don't leave."

THE VIGIL IN THE ICU

Tuesday. The cab driver and I were a little confused as to which hospital. There were two, one in Ft. Walton Beach and one in Niceville but it was a different name than Alex had told me. He drove me to the one in Niceville and waited outside while I ran in to see if Carole was there. It was a small hospital. My stomach sank as I rushed in because I was already thinking about what kind of ICU a small hospital like this could support. The woman at the information desk already had eye contact with me before I reached the desk. "Yes" she said immediately, "She's here."

I ran back to the cab, got my suitcase and thanked the cab driver. I realized he was exceptionally nice. I moved quickly through the lobby and people came out of nowhere and pointed me in the right direction. ICU was at the opposite corner of the hospital but only a three or four minute walk. In between there were glass doors leading to courtyards where people were milling around or sitting at outdoor tables. I found room 120 across the hall from the ICU entrance (which had signs saying not to come in, but to call on the house phone for permission to enter and the times when this was permissible.)

The three days we sat vigil for Carole at the Niceville Hospital have turned into a blur except for a few scenes that stand out in my memory. One thing I know and all of us who were there said this repeatedly, "The people here *are* so *nice*. *This*   is unbelievable."

They gave us a semi-private (patient) room (room 120) to stay in immediately across from the entrance to the Intensive Care Unit. This is unheard of at other hospitals. Everyone on the hospital staff was totally there for us.

The other thing that stands out in my memory and embraces my heart is that Alex's relatives that were there told me over and over how much Carole loved me. They knew so much about me from her and they were sincerely grateful for the positive changes they saw in her, and they said it was because of Charlie and me. I guess I was overwhelmed by all this because I just loved Carole. That was enough for me. She so willingly accepted my love, and she was easy to love. This idea began to grow in my head and heart. I loved Carole in a way most people couldn't accept. Most people I guess, don't feel worthy or something. On the other hand, she openly accepted me and my love and gave it back in return. This relationship we had came so easily that I guess I never noticed or paid much attention to how rare it was. Not until I realized I was losing Carole. We were all losing her.

Alex took me in to the intensive care unit. I had prepared myself, having worked in an ICU years before. He left me alone with her, as my eyes became accustomed to finding her under all the tubes and lines. I lifted one eyelid and then the other. Her pupils were large and fixed. She was motionless. My heart sunk. I held her hand. My heart talked to hers, because I knew she was watching and listening. She might not be in her body, but I knew she was there. Alex came back into the cubicle and for his sake and mine I said to her," Carole there's a shoe sale at Nordstrom's. Come on Honey, wake up. We have to move fast."

Alex laughed. I laughed. We talked about how we knew she was going to come out of this. Alex bent over her --close to her ear and said, "Carole, open your eyes and I promise that I'm going to buy you the biggest diamond ring." She didn't move.

I thought to myself, "She's young and besides -- she's strong. She's going to come out of this."

Alex's brother Tony, his sister Karen and his mother Eileen were there. We were out in the courtyard often, visiting and warming up because the hospital was kept so cold. Carole's parents and her sister were there too. Her parents stayed mainly in the ICU waiting room and we were in room 120 or the courtyard. Occasionally one or more of us walked around the outside of the building. Sometimes, as I walked alone, I could see Alex walking either with Tony or alone--or Karen walking with her Mom a few feet ahead or behind. Once while I was coming in as I passed the door to the ICU, Carole's parents were about to come out and I overheard her mother say to her husband, "What a shame to see someone that out of control."

"What an odd statement," I thought. Then I remembered all the times Carole had talked about her mother only caring about appearances. I remembered her words exactly and where we were sitting. We were in the coffee place near my house and she said, "I have talked to other women who have been sexually abused, and we all know our 'co-abusers' are only concerned about appearances..." With Carole's urging -- Charlie had even started looking at the traits of co-abusers for a research article. Carole also wanted to know how alcoholism contributed to the way her mother and other children of alcoholics acted when confronted. Now I heard her mother talk about 'the shame of being out of control.' I wanted to discuss this with Carole. I told myself to wait until she was all healed and then tell her.

I found Alex sitting alone in room 120. I looked in his eyes and said, "Alex, you look so exhausted. What can I do to help you?" Alex suggested that we meditate. He felt like he was "all over the place" and thought meditation might help him.

Alex sat cross-legged on the bed near the door. I relaxed on the hospital bed next to the window and prayed for Carole, and then said a prayer for all of us who had gathered around her and finally I said my usual prayer before meditation. Twenty minutes or so flew by and I quietly got up and sat in the big arm chair at the foot of Alex's bed. He looked at me with a half smile and said, "I keep going over that scene at the motel when Carole collapsed. She was still in pain. She knew she was going to die. She told me. Then she said 'good-bye.' I called the hospital where we had gone the day before. I told you didn't I? -- that we went in and they x-rayed her and they told us she was only constipated-- that there was a blockage, and they gave her a laxative. So I called them back and asked them to give her pain medication but they said they couldn't. It would counter the effects of the laxative."

"I was on the phone at the time and I heard Carole speak and I looked over as she said, 'Alex, I'm dying. I'll love you forever. Good-bye.' I turned around and saw her collapsed on the floor. I knew her body was lifeless. I started CPR -- I only stopped long enough to call for help. The EMTs came just a few minutes later. What could I have done differently?"

"Alex," I said, hoping he would lift his eyes and look at me, "Do you know about "survivor guilt?"

And then there was a loud knock on the door. It opened enough for Carole's parents to see me sitting in the chair.

Alex said to them firmly, "We'll be out in a few minutes."

The door closed and then there was silence for a few seconds. Then in his soft voice Alex continued to navigate the rough waters he had been wading through since this catastrophic scene had begun.

Two minutes later, there was another loud knock on the door. I walked to the door and opened it part way. Carole's mother pushed in as far as I would let the door go. She said, "It's time. We want to go in and see Carole. Where's Alex?" Then they pushed far enough that they could see him on the bed.

Carole's father looked at me and said with a threatening force in his voice, "Are you a therapist? Are you my daughter's therapist? Are you one of those RMT therapists?" (He was referring to a term the accused child molesters had made up, 'recovered memory therapy.' Actually, there is no such kind of therapy.)

I took a step backward because his rage --or what had just happened-- cut in to me. It felt as though a missile or torpedo had somehow psychically shot into me and then had exploded.

I was shaking violently inside...

As he continued speaking *at* me, I couldn't understand his words, but could sense this panorama of all the innocent children who were abused by someone like him... I was an adult. I could walk away whereas a child, indeed his own daughters, so dependent on him, couldn't escape the pain of his continual sexual assaults. As I became more aware of the trembling going on inside my body, I realized that what the children were up against was bigger-- more hurtful than anything I could have imagined before... My mother had physically abused me out of ignorance and her frustration and anger over her own childhood. This man's verbal assault had a toxic power to it that was bigger than I had ever felt before.

Whatever it was he shot at me, I was so torn open after just hearing Alex's description of Carole's collapse that I took in this man's rage. I was totally consumed. I remember stammering, denying I was her therapist, telling them that Carole and I were friends. His wife said to me through the door, "But you are working with her. We know you are working together." Her attitude was as though her 34-year-old daughter should not be working with me or anyone else.

"Yes, on a documentary..." I was still stammering and shaking when I heard Alex say in a powerful voice to them, "Close the door and wait for me in the ICU waiting room. I'll be out in awhile."

I don't remember what happened next. But I was alone, walking in the hall. There was no one I knew around. I trembled at an even harder rate now, feeling as though my insides had been kicked out of me and telling myself that this whole scene was about Carole's parents, not about me or my history with these people who have been accused by both their daughters of sexually abusing them as children. I didn't want to draw attention to myself or this scene.

My knees were like jelly. I kept walking. I walked for quite a while. I finally saw Tony in the cafeteria. His very size started to calm me a little.

A voice inside of me said, "If you want to stay here to be with Carole-- you need to tell him. You need to tell someone. You need to know someone will protect you. Tell Tony!"

Without going into too much detail, I told him what had just happened. I asked for him to keep an eye on them and me. I told him I needed to feel that I had someone to protect me from that hostile man. He understood and agreed, saying now he knew there was a purpose in his coming. I thought: how strange that was, because as far as I was concerned, Tony had already taken on so much responsibility here. Usually in scenes like this, I took on all the responsibility, but I had gladly stepped aside when he moved in to handle everything. And he did it well. There is a wonderful presence about Tony. I'm glad that I told him.

Mid-afternoon, we all gathered in room 120. Instead of sitting in the ICU waiting room, Carole's parents and sister came into the room, also. Someone answered the phone. Charlie was calling. I was on with him briefly telling him that nothing was new and I would call him back later.

Carole's mother asked loudly to the whole room, "Charlie? Whitfield? What kind of a doctor is he?"

"Internist. Internal Medicine." I said because Charlie had actually started out in internal medicine 35 years ago. I shuddered at the thought of her figuring out that Charlie was the Charles Whitfield who had written *Memory and Abuse* exposing the falsies' disinformation to the public.

The phone rang again and Alex was now talking to someone long distance.

The rest of us were quiet and Mrs. F turned to me and half said, half asked, "I need to talk to you when this is all over. I want to know about Carole. I have missed seven years of my daughter's life. I have this big hole in my knowledge of my daughter. I know you can tell me. I need to have your phone number."

I didn't know what to say. I knew she wasn't fully aware of who Charlie was-- and when she finally put that information together, well, I just didn't want to be there!

"Tell me about the documentary. Tell me what you are doing with them... Please!' she almost pleaded.

"About the documentary?" I tried to be pleasant as I answered her with, "It's based on a conference I chaired last year. It's hard to explain... We are looking at the Eastern medical model of energy... like the energy used in acupuncture. We know that it works, but here in the West we don't accept or use it. Our religions talk around it. But neither our religions or our medical model incorporate it into our model of health.   Carole and Alex interviewed all these great minds that came to speak and they are putting together a wonderfully spiritual documentary. It's not religious, but spiritual."

I wondered if I'd said too much.

At that point, Alex-- still on the phone, gave me a look that was easy to read. He wanted me to stop talking about it, and I did. Eileen picked up the conversation. Mr. F looked almost deflated and didn't say anything. In fact, he never said another word in front of me.

Alex told me later, "You can't tell what these people will do with any information you give them. And I don't want them hanging out with us in room 120. They should stay in the ICU waiting room. We don't have to bring them into our circle. I know it's not easy to think that way because they are parents who are suffering too, but we're not embracing them. We are allowing them to be here to finish their unfinished business with Carole. I know she would want it that way.

THAT EVENING

Dr. Reeve, the gynecologist who operated on Carole, and the neurologist came in to talk to all of us in room 120. They believed, from the tests they had run, that Carole may be brain dead. We asked questions and both physicians patiently answered.

Afterward, I walked outside in the moonlight to be alone with my tears... Suddenly, all the lawn sprinklers turned on. There were long streams of water shooting everywhere. No matter which way I turned, I got soaked...

A few minutes later, I sat in room 120 trembling from the wet and the air-conditioning, plus the decision we were all being asked to make with Alex and Tony. Dr. Reeve sat with us two other difficult times and explained all the implications. Her face flushed, she sat with us and cried, too. She said her work was usually "happy medicine" and so Carole's condition was affecting her too. She said this was the scenario that all obstetricians dreaded. There's often no way to tell the diagnosis of ruptured ectopic pregnancy until the patient was dead. Surgery was usually too late. There was just no way to tell that the pregnancy had connected outside the uterus between the fallopian tube and the top of the uterus. This was called a "Corneal Pregnancy."(near the tubal opening onto the uterus.) People with this condition commonly bled to death. Even though heroic measures were performed to get Carole's heart going again, her body was alive only from the neck down. There was no blood being pumped up to her brain during CPR. Her brain had died from lack of blood flow when she bled so heavily into her abdominal cavity.

Did we accept the conclusion that Carole's brain was dead or did we transfer her to a hospital that was a bigger and more sophisticated facility? There would be more sophisticated technology plus a bigger staff of specialists. Tony was talking about Northside Hospital in Atlanta which is close to Charlie and my house. I became alive again, excited. I told him which doctors to call. I also thought we should call Charlie and let him work from that end. We all agreed and Tony said he would investigate the whole procedure.

My thoughts were so frantic, my heart so heavy-- I knew I didn't want to be alone. So Carole's sister, Alex's mother, Eileen and his sister Karen, and I had all agreed to share a room that night. We agreed we would go to a restaurant first and then the Comfort Inn where we had a room with two double beds.

We stood in the hospital lobby waiting for a cab that would take 45 minutes or longer to arrive, since it was already after 9pm in this sleepy little town called 'Niceville'. Karen called the Comfort Inn and asked if they would pick us up because she had noticed a van they had for airport runs. The woman at the desk picked us up in five minutes and took us to a trendy little restaurant near the motel. Eileen tried to pay her but she wouldn't accept any money.

We ate together and our mood picked up because, after all, there still was hope. There was the big city hospital to which we would take Carole. We had seen so many movies, especially when we were younger where the heroine opened her eyes after many days in a coma and says, "Where am I?" We painted that scene over and over in our conversation. We were amazed by the fact that the young woman from the motel wouldn't take any money for driving us. People really were nice in Niceville. To prove our point, we asked if any of the restaurant staff could drive us back to the motel because we were warned this was not a safe highway to walk along. A young man instantly offered to take us. He too, would not accept any money. He said that was how people are in Niceville.

An hour later, as we tried to relax in the motel room, I told Eileen and Karen that Carole had purposely brought us to Niceville to show us that there still were some peaceful and kind areas in the world. (Lately I had been down on the violence and unkindness of our species. While in Niceville I was changing my mind.)

Alex's mom, Eileen said, "Not only did Carole bring us to 'Niceville', did you hear where she collapsed?"

"No." I said, "And, knowing Carole, this has got to be good."

"She collapsed in 'Destin!' You know, like she was '*destin*' to be there!"

"Oh! I get it! I get it!

"By the way, where is Carole's sister? She disappeared when we came back here."

Eileen answered, "She went to her parent's room to tell her father she forgave him. Now it was his turn. She wanted him to apologize to Carole in the morning. She's telling him that because Carole is in a coma-- this might be his last chance."

She came in hours later. She said she had pleaded with him. Although he never agreed, she did come back to our room feeling elated because she felt the chances were good that he would apologize to Carole in the morning.

Wednesday Of course, someone from the Comfort Inn drove us back to the Niceville Hospital. Eileen didn't try tipping anymore. By now we accepted everyone's kindness.

We gathered in Room 120 and waited for Tony and Alex to come in. We waited and waited. Finally Tony came in alone and told us he had made all the plans to move Carole. During that time on the phone late last night he had also talked to specialists in New Jersey and elsewhere. They told him they agreed with the doctors here-- that there wasn't even a 1% chance of Carole coming out of the coma. All tests indicated she was brain dead. He was now reversing the idea of taking her somewhere else and wanted us to realize that eventually we would have to all decide together to allow the staff to pronounce Carole dead. Until we did, if her heart gave out, the staff would be compelled to resuscitate her, and not only wouldn't that help, it was painful to think about. The other thing was that Alex had remembered that Carole had wanted her organs donated and the longer we waited, the more the possibility that that would become more difficult.

"Where was Alex?" we asked. And Tony told us he would be coming along soon, but that he was naturally taking all this very hard and needed to gather his strength to come back.

Dr. Reeve came in again and talked and cried with us. The neurologist stood in the corner near the door and supported her continuing explanations. Alex came in and everyone stayed strong. We talked. I don't remember anymore what was said. It was a blur until a staff person came in to explain the organ donor procedure. I couldn't comprehend all that-- or just blocked it-- because I didn't need to understand at that moment.

We would have all day to say good-bye to Carole. There were no more time restrictions placed on us. We could go in to ICU as we pleased.

I walked in to see her a few more times. Once, around 2pm, when I was alone with her, I drew the curtains and said my real good-bye. I laid my hands on her as I had done so many times before-- to do a healing-- and I prayed. I prayed that she heard me. I prayed for her to be free and with God. I prayed for Alex. I told her, I don't know how many times, that I loved her. I played with her hair. I held her hand. I took off her socks and massaged her feet one more time. They were so crusted over with eczema. I promised her that her feet would never bother her again. I thought about how no matter how much she had healed emotionally and psychologically from her childhood sexual abuse, her hands and feet still carried the pain. One time later in the day when I was saying good-bye again, I kissed her foot because I couldn't get to her face. All the tubes were in the way. I tried to tell myself and her that lots of people were going to live now because she had died. I didn't go in when Daniel, the priest gave her the last rites.

I was sitting alone in the courtyard and Eileen sat down across the table from me.

"I don't believe it," she said. "I was in the cafeteria and Carole's parents came in and sat down with me. I started talking to them and... I can't remember a thing that I said but I know it was profound... I think... I think the Holy Spirit was talking through me.

"I could tell by the look on their faces that they understood every word. It was the most amazing thing..."

Alex suggested that Carole's parents go in to the Intensive Care Unit and say their good-byes to her and then come back in to room 120, because he wanted to speak to them alone. Tony had told Alex that even if his talk with them didn't go well, at least there would be closure and he could "direct traffic", by directing them from the hospital.

They returned full of emotion, sobbing, eyes glazed over, burning red. The two sat on the hospital bed while Carole's sister sat in a chair, with a look of bewilderment.

Alex was standing. He said, "I would like to try and talk to you all on behalf of Carole. I've known her extremely well over the past seven years.

"First of all-- Carole loved each of you very much."

Carole's father said, "I know she did."

Her mother said, "We loved her very much."

Her father said, "Let him talk."

Alex said: "Yes, I'd like to speak and have you listen. When I'm done, you can ask any questions."

Both parents answered, "Okay."

Alex said, "Carole was about love. She lived in love and truth. She was able to turn sexual abuse into a blessing in her life and live in forgiveness. She wanted you to be a family and she wanted you to help her sister. If you truly would like to honor her life you will live in love-- not fear. You will take it one step at a time and give up your need for control and live in truth now.

"Carole gave each of you gifts before she died. She gave you, her mother, spirituality and her father... she gave you truth. These are real gifts, if you focus on those in your lives you will heal. As always, though it's up to each of you. You each have free will and need to choose to heal each day.

"Carole languished endlessly over the tragedy in your family. She wanted nothing more than for you to be a family, heal and protect each other as a family. But now you have to live in truth.

"She wanted you two to help her sister and her sister's children. Tragically *she* is your only daughter now. You need to take care of her. And you need to help her children heal, too. Take it one step at a time. Create healthy boundaries. It's going to be difficult but you can do it.

"It's up to you. I'm trying to speak for Carole, I have mixed feelings about the whole thing. If you can do this, you would give real meaning to her death. She is watching over you and wants you to choose love-- not fear.

"I think that's it. I hope you will really think about what I'm saying and when you leave start to make it happen."

Her mother spoke first. "Well, last night we started and when we leave we are going to keep working at it."

Her father said, "I'm in."

Her mother said, "We would like for you to come visit us and tell us about your life with Carole. We've missed the last seven years of your life."

Alex answered, "I would visit you only if you are a family living in truth. If you look for God you will find truth and love for each other. I wish you luck. Nothing would make me happier than to see Carole's wishes come true. God bless you."

And Alex walked them to the door of 120 and shut it after they were out so he could be alone.

I was in the front lobby near the desk as Carole's parents and sister were coming out to leave. I took a deep breath and asked God for help. I then addressed her mother. "You asked to be able to contact me later because you said you haven't known your daughter in seven years. You said there is a big hole missing for you in her life and you wanted me to fill you in. Well, if you are ready, I am willing to do it now."

She nodded and silently followed me into the cafeteria. I was grateful it was practically empty. We sat at the first table across from each other. I looked her directly in the eye and said, "I want you to know that Carole did an amazing amount of healing and growing in the three or so years I knew her. She healed from her childhood abuse as much as is possible and then she moved on and grew so much spiritually that it was a wonderful pleasure to watch her."

Her mother said, "You mean she became self-actualized."

"Yes, that and so much more." I answered. "She became connected spiritually. Self actualized is all about psychological growth-- which Carole did. But she studied and prayed and worked on the documentary and became directly connected -- not to any one religion but directly to Spirit and to her Self.

"There was so much joy in her. It was obvious to all of us that she and Alex were meant for each other. They were good companions. They supported each other's work. And they loved each other deeply. As she healed she became joyful in her everyday living. And even the little things gave her pleasure.

"Did you know she had a near-death experience?"

She shook her head no.

"Well, that probably connected her spiritually, and she continued learning and growing at an incredible rate. She even told her near-death experience on a TV show in Canada."

I saw a look come over her mother's face that perhaps only mothers of grown daughters can understand. Mother-daughter relationships in 'normal' families are complex, let alone one as muddied as this one, but her look said a million words, or perhaps is beyond describing.

She then said, "Carole was so talented. She was always talented."

"Yes she was and I just want you to know that Carole was happy and full of creative endeavors. Her talents were being aimed in all the right directions. She felt fulfilled and she and Alex shared so much joy."

And, that was it. It all ended as abruptly as it began.

Eileen and I watched as they left the building and walked across the parking lot. Carole's father walked ahead, with his wife a few steps behind and finally their daughter walking alone. They all had slumped heads and shoulders. Eileen and I said a prayer for the three of them.

Alex was standing behind me watching them walk away too. Eileen went to make a phone call and Alex and I walked quietly back toward the ICU. He hesitated for a moment and faced me as we walked. I stopped too and as we faced each other he said, "You know, Barbara. We are walking through a movie."

"I know, Alex. I know..."

And it finally sunk in and we fully acknowledged the fact that this lifetime was over for Carole and all that was left for us to do was give permission to pronounce her dead.

Many of the hospital staff cried with us. The ICU staff was upset and crying. The woman at the information desk cried. I sat alone in the lobby, crying and the night security guard walked up to me and when he heard it was 34 year old Carole who I was crying for-- he cried, too. He actually sat on the arm of a big lounge chair across from me and tears came to his eyes. I watched them roll down his cheeks. He prayed for her at his church meeting the night before. She was so young and he wanted to believe there would be a miracle. He stayed a few minutes and then continued his rounds.

Alex, Eileen, Karen and I had briefly mentioned to each other the sense of something spiritual encompassing us, or was it the hospital? No, it had to be Niceville. We were grateful for whatever was happening to us because we knew very well we were in a horrific experience, too. But we felt watched and cared for. I remember a few mentions of angels and of course we knew Carole was there. There was this peace that pervaded the hospital and spread out to wherever we were-- motel or restaurant. Even sleeping had a quality that isn't usually there. We were bathed in it. Somehow we were anesthetized against the agony we knew was coming. We were in pain but it was bearable because we had a sense of being enveloped by an indefinable gentleness.

Carole was finishing this lifetime. However, she was doing it without any chance to say good-bye. No one could say anything to her-- at least not to her body. So I was continually talking to her in my heart. The others were too. The strange part was that we heard or understood her answers and sometimes we would even chuckle. She had an amazing sense of humor.

Robin Reeve asked to see a picture of Carole because she had only seen her with swollen face and tubes and lines everywhere. I got a beautiful picture from Carole's purse of her and Alex staring into each others eyes at their wedding only five years earlier. I showed it to Robin and she cried with me in the cafeteria.

"Who will look out for him now-- during this time??" she asked. "Does he have a support system back home?"

I answered. "My husband is a physician and psychotherapist, but more, he is Alex's friend. We live close by. We'll take care of him."

She sighed and her face softened. She touched my shoulder and said, "Thank you."

Others came in to talk to her, so I took the picture of Carole and Alex and went back to the ICU. I watched as the staff passed the picture around. Each looked at it with shock or denial. "So young, so young. You'll have to excuse us but we hardly ever see anyone in this unit that dies so young."

"Me neither." I said as I walked back to Carole's corner with my chin almost on my chest. It didn't help my pain to stand there with her anymore. She had been pronounced dead and although that didn't change the ventilator's breathing for her, I now understood that what was being done-- was now being done to keep her organs alive for other people. Her body didn't contain Carole anymore, and I felt like I could get closer to her at home alone, in prayer or sitting by the water somewhere-- more than I could here with this shell. She had such a big Soul and this wasn't her anymore. The last thing I said as I stood there looking at her body was, "Carole, my love, whoever receives your heart will be an incredibly fortunate person!"

DINNER IN DESTIN

We walked out of the hospital quietly, Alex, Tony, Eileen, Karen and me. We were in such a daze that at first we had trouble finding the car. We just wandered through the parking lot until we finally recognized Tony's rental car. I was between Eileen and Karen in the back -- Tony drove and Alex sat in the passenger seat. I watched the panorama through the windows as Niceville passed us by. I had no idea where we were going nor did I care. No one spoke. K-Marts, Walmarts, fast food restaurants slid by. Alex finally broke the silence with, "Tony, put on the radio."

Elton John was singing, 'Daniel, You're the One.' The priest who had just given Carole the last rites was named Daniel. The lyrics continued having relevance.

Alex changed the station. "Where ever you go, what ever you do, I will be right here waiting for you..." And it repeated over and over...

"Alex," I said. "Are you listening to the words? First Daniel and now this."

"Yeah!" he said, "She's here." He spoke so softly and then he sobbed.

We drove for about 40 minutes until we saw the beaches of Destin. We passed the hotel where they were when she collapsed. And Alex told us all about how Carole wanted to walk on the beach. Choking up he said, "I had suggested Sunday morning that we drive back home, but she said 'no' because she was hoping she would be feeling better and that evening we would walk the beaches of Destin."

Tony pulled into the parking lot of a beautiful weathered-looking seafood restaurant that was on the Gulf of Mexico. We walked in. My legs carried me, but my body didn't feel attached to them. We sat in a booth looking out through a huge window that was wide open to a spectacular panoramic view of the Gulf , white sand beaches, fishing boats, pelicans and gulls soaring and calling. We ordered dinner. Mine tasted awful, but I knew it wasn't the chef's fault. We made arrangements for the trip back to Atlanta the next day. Karen, Alex and Tony flew. Eileen and I drove Carole's car back.

THE NEXT DAY

It was good that Eileen and I were alone together for the six hour ride back-- Two women, the same age telling each other our life story. I enjoyed her company even through the heavy grief we were both feeling. We pulled into Alex and Carole's carport only minutes after Alex, Tony and Karen arrived from the airport. As we hugged hello we marveled at the timing. We drove for 6 hours, their flight was an hour. It didn't figure, but we gave it up. All we knew was that we were in some kind of space-time warp. It started in Niceville and I had explained it to myself first and then to Karen and Eileen as being a spiritual experience that we were all in. It is common during the death of a loved one to feel as though time is transcended and there is a sense of connectedness beyond this reality. Karen had already found Carole's copy of my book *Spiritual Awakenings,* and she was carrying it around and saying, "Yeah! Here it is—having a Spiritual experience during the death of a loved one."

Charlie came over to get me and sat for a while with Alex. We were exhausted, so Charlie and I agreed we would come back in the morning. The four of them weren't flying out until 2 o'clock the next afternoon. Eileen was going back to Arizona. Alex, Tony and Karen were going to New Jersey where they were planning a memorial service for family and friends the next weekend. I knew it was going to be hard to say good-bye in the morning. We would be splitting to three different parts of the country and splitting the group in this shared spiritual experience of saying good-bye to a Soul we all loved dearly. Now the longer grieving process would begin. I would have to face my pain alone. I would come face to face with losing Carole.

CHAPTER 10

HONORING CAROLE

When Charlie and I walked in the next morning, Alex asked us to come into the bedroom and he shut the door so we could be alone. He looked at us and in a soft voice said, "I want you both to come to New Jersey to the memorial service. I need you both there. Please, will you both come and help me honor Carole?"

Charlie and I looked at each other, and like two parents who know they can't refuse their child, we both said, "Yes."

And then we asked Alex what he had said to Carole's parents before they left the hospital. He told us, and we were both astonished-- at his courage and his wisdom and the appropriateness of what he said.

"Alex, that was so good. I hope and pray that they understood. Can you write that all out? We need to have that in print. We need to somehow get it published so that other parents can read what you said. We need to protect their identity but we also need to share all that wisdom with other parents who have been rightly accused of child sexual abuse."

Alex said, again in a soft voice, "I'll write it out today, before we leave. But you've got to know that when I was talking to Carole's parents, it wasn't me. I thought I was talking *for* Carole, but now I realize that it could have been Carole talking...

The following Friday afternoon, Charlie and I flew to Newark. Tony picked us up and drove us to his home for dinner. I was glad to see Eileen. Tony and his wife, Nina sent her a plane ticket, insisting that she needed to be with all of us. Alex's aunt and uncle, Jean and Tom came for dinner, too. After dinner, they were taking us and Eileen to their home for the night.

As Nina and Tony were preparing to serve a delicious Italian dinner she told me a story that gave me goose bumps. It seems that her sister, this week-- one week to the day after Carole collapsed in the hotel room-- went to the hospital in terrific pain. She was in her fourth month of pregnancy and her husband, who is a physician, and the doctors there couldn't figure out what was wrong. Then Nina, frantic with fear and still reeling from Carole's tragedy, insisted that they check her for an ectopic pregnancy. It *was* an ectopic pregnancy and she was bleeding. They caught it just in time to save her life. I shook my head and said, "You and Carole just saved a life." Tears were coming into my eyes and rolling down my cheeks. Nina's eyes were tearing up too. Standing in the kitchen over chafing dishes of pasta-- we pulled ourselves out of our pain because we both needed to function. We were in a kind of overload that we both understood...

Jean and Tom live on a lake. We arrived way after dark. Except for a few lights out on the other side of the lake, we really couldn't see its beauty. So the five of us sat together around the kitchen table and talked for a while. Then Charlie and I excused ourselves and went to bed. We were exhausted and knew tomorrow was going to be a hard day.

I awakened at 3:00 am, worrying about what I was going to say and still in shock about the fact that Carole was gone. I wanted to talk to her. I wanted her to know that I had dinner at Tony's and Nina's. She had told me about them and I wanted to talk to her about Tony and Nina's kids. Carole had told me about Susan, their oldest daughter. I wanted to tell her she was right. Susan was a great kid. I wanted to tell Carole we were with Jean and Tom, and that they were everything she had said. I didn't want to be going to a memorial service for Carole. I wanted to be with her.

I tossed and turned until 4:30. Then I gave up. I got out of bed, searching for my robe. I tip toed down the stairs in the dark and found my way to the sun room. I planned on sitting there until the sun came up. I had no idea which side of the lake we were facing but when the sun came up I knew it would be a beautiful sight to see. I needed to see something good. The sun coming up might give me a sense of renewal-- a symbol that life starts fresh again every day. I walked into the room with a small lamp lit. I went to sit by the window and was a little surprised when I heard a man's voice say to me,   "Don't let me startle you."

"Oh, you couldn't sleep either?" I said to Tom, and this was the beginning of a two hour conversation that I will always treasure. You know, there are those moments in life when you just know...

A few minutes into the conversation, I took a deep breath and relaxed into what was happening. I stopped worrying about what I would be like if I didn't get back to sleep and I just enjoyed Tom's stories. He gave me a jacket to wear over my robe because the windows were open in the room-- and there's a cold dampness before dawn on a lake. I curled up in one of his kid's jackets, leaning against the arm of an over-stuffed chair and sure enough, the sun came up on the other side of the lake so I could watch it rise in the sky and also in the lake's reflection. And, as the sun came up, the sleeping birds awoke and I heard them sing their glorious good morning songs.

Tom told me about Carole and Alex's wedding. The reception had been on this lake at a club house close by.

The best story Tom told I'll remember for ever. He said, "I knew this man most of my life. He was quite a bit older than me. He died just two years ago in his mid-eighties.

"He was drafted during World War II. At that time our government believed the Japanese would invade Australia so my friend was sent there.

"He had a loving, close marriage to this wonderful young woman. They did almost everything together. They were married a short time, less than three years when he was sent to Australia and while he was there she was killed in a car accident. But he wasn't allowed to come home for her funeral because our troops couldn't leave for fear of invasion.

"After the war ended, after he finally came home, he had psychological problems for a short while. He was a positive person. He never complained. He held everything in. I never heard him say anything about his pain or this woman he adored. But he couldn't go back to the mountains where they had lived. I knew him for more than 50 years and he never said anything.

"A few years later he remarried and had another happy marriage. They walked together, they did everything together. They were married for over 50 years. Then she developed Alzheimer's and went into a nursing home where he was always with her until she died.

"Once, Jean and I went to visit her in the home. After the visit we went with him for coffee. Let me just back up a little here and tell you that my father had just died and he had come to our house where we took care of him until he died. He left us all his pictures and I was putting them together in an album when I ran across a picture of this man with his first wife. That picture started me thinking and I told him about it over coffee. Then I got up the nerve to ask him, 'Do you ever think about her?'

And this man who never shared what he held inside, said to me 'Every single day of my life...'

Isn't that something? I realized the depth of people. He went on and lived his life but never lost the depth of love and all the sadness that he carried. He went on with his life. Yet he never betrayed his love for his first wife and he lived every day. And his words, 'Every single day of my life' continue to echo in my ears..."

Tom's story gave me hope that Alex would come through the loss of Carole, his "Soul-twin."

DRIVE TO SPRING LAKE

Around 10 in the morning, we left for the two hour drive to Spring Lake, on New Jersey's Atlantic Shore. Jean drove and we tried our best to keep the conversation going but there were many silences, too. We knew this was emotionally and spiritually huge. All of us had adored Carole. All of us were going to her Memorial Service...

About half way there Tom asked me to read what I was going to say at the service. My first thought was that it would be good to say it out loud. But then I thought I was sitting in the back middle seat and all I could see was the back of Jean and Tom's heads and the highway ahead of us. I told him it would be hard for me because I couldn't see their faces like I can when I talk to a group.

"That's all right, Barbara. Go ahead and read it anyway. I would like to hear it. We may miss hearing you because we have to leave early." And I remembered that they had an evening wedding at West Point, three hours away.

I unfolded my papers and checked to see if they were in order.

"Okay, but bear with me. I don't know...

"Let me start by saying that what I am about to read comes from my last book *Final Passage.* This was written by me but with Carole's help. I read her my description of my near-death experience and she added her memories of what she felt when she was held by God-- as she felt God in her near-death experience. Whatever she said-- I added, so this is from the two of us...

"Now I felt God's love, this love was holding me. It felt incredible. There are no words in the English language, or maybe in this reality, to explain the kind of love God emanates. God was *totally accepting* of everything we-- God and I, reviewed in my life........

"In every scene of my life review I could feel again what I had felt at various times in my life. And I could feel everything everyone else felt as a consequence of my actions. Some of it felt good and some of it felt awful. All of this translated into knowledge, *and I learned-- oh, how I learned!* ....

"The information was flowing at an incredible breakneck speed that probably would have burned me up if it weren't for the extraordinary Energy holding me. The information came in, and then love neutralized my judgments against myself. In other words, information about every scene-- my perceptions and feelings-- and anyone else's perceptions and feelings that were in the scene came to me... No matter how I judged myself in each interaction, being held by God was the bigger interaction. God interjected love into everything, every feeling, every bit of information about absolutely everything that went on, so that everything was all right. There was no good and no bad. There was only me and my loved ones from this life trying to be, or just trying to survive.

"I realize now that without God holding me, I wouldn't have had the strength to experience what I did.

"When it started, God and I were merging, we became one-- so that I could see through God's eyes and feel through God's heart. We, together, witnessed how severely I had treated myself because that was the behavior shown and taught to me as a child. I realized that the only big mistake I made in my life of thirty-two years was that I never learned to love myself.....

"I also realized that we don't end at our skin. We are all in this big churning mass of consciousness. We are each a part of this consciousness we call God. we're not just human. We are Spirit. We were Spirit before we came into this lifetime. We are all struggling Spirits now, trying to get "being human" right. And when we leave here, we will be pure Spirit again.

'God held me and let me into God's experience of all this. I felt God's memories of these scenes through God's eyes. I could sense God's divine intelligence and it was astonishing. God loves us and wants us to learn and wake up to our real selves-- to what is important. I realized that *God wants us to know that we only experience real pain if we die without living first.* And the way to live is to give love to ourselves and to others.   'Frommy experience, and from what I heard from Carole's experience, it seems that we are here to learn to give and receive love. But only when we heal enough to be real can we understand and give and receive love the way love was meant to be.

'When God held Carole and God held me in our life reviews and we merged into one, we remember this feeling as being limitless. God is limitless. God's capacity to love is never-ending. God's love for us never changes no matter how we are. God doesn't judge us either. During our life review, *we judge ourselves when we feel the pain we have created in other's lives.*

"Carole and I never saw an old man with a white beard sitting in judgment of us. We only felt limitless divine love.

"God, as Carole and I experienced God, only gives. God interjected love into all the scenes of our lives to show us God's reality. And the most amazing part of all is that God held nothing back. We understood all that God understood. God let us in. God shared all of Godself with us-- all the qualities of gentleness and openness, and all the gifts......... including our own empowerment and peace. We never knew that much loving intelligence and freedom could exist. God held us in eternity.

"I am back here, in time, but still with God. It is just a little harder for me to realize God's presence because my body and my mind get in the way. But that's all right. I still feel It. Especially when I think of the Love Carole and I shared....

"I think of Carole and her strength and her love of life and her zest for healing and those memories bring me closer to feeling what Carole and I felt in our near-death experiences...

"I was privileged to watch Carole healing from the darkest of child abuse and then soar into all kinds of spiritual growth. She knew that as we awaken to what is real- not the physical world that only teaches us to achieve and consume-- but the real world where our spirits grow and learn about healing and love ---we awaken to our own Soul. She knew that as we awaken we will find our Soul family. And I feel we are Soul family with Carole and Alex."

When I finished no one said anything. I was afraid to ask if it was okay so I just sat there watching the road. Finally, Tom's voice broke the silence with, "Would you read that again, please." So I did.

CAROLE'S MEMORIAL SERVICE

As we drove through Spring Lake toward the ocean, I realized that this must have been a wonderful place for Carole and Alex to date during their first summer together. We parked in front of the hotel where they stayed. It was a quaint white clapboard Inn overlooking the Atlantic. We gathered for a luncheon and then the service, which would be led by Alex. Several of us were to speak, including Carole's sister (who was here without her parents). I was deeply grieving and numb at the same time.

Charlie and I walked into the banquet room overlooking the ocean. It was actually divided into two areas and the first had several tables set up with flowers, candles and numerous pictures of Carole. There was thirty-four years of Carole in framed pictures. Seven of those years showed pictures of Carole and Alex smiling through dates, through their wedding, on Good Morning America with Diane Sawyer and at our house. I couldn't look at them at first. I sat down at a window and just looked out. Eventually, I was able to go back and study all the pictures-- a few at a time.

Alex even brought the aura picture of Carole from the front of their refrigerator. I smiled as I thought of us at Whole Life

Expo-- didgeridoos, aura pictures and even psychics saying, 'Diane Sawyer.'

People we had never met walked up to Charlie and me and told us, "She loved you two so much. She always talked about you."

We met the rest of Alex's family. 80 people came. Many were Carole and Alex's age and several had infants with them. After an excellent meal, Alex began the memorial with all of us moving our chairs into the area where we were surrounded by candles burning on the tables filled with Carole's pictures and flowers. He stood next to a television and VCR.

Alex, sad but composed, welcomed us and then said, "If you will all get together and join hands with the persons next to you, I would like to start with a prayer:

"Our Father Who Art in Heaven, Hallowed Be Thy Name. Thy Kingdom Come, Thy Will Be Done, On Earth as it is in Heaven. Give us this day our daily bread, and forgive us our trespasses as we forgive those who trespass against us. Lead us not into temptation, but deliver us from all evil. For Thine is the kingdom, the power and the glory, now and forever.

"Dear God please bring the Holy Spirit into each of us right now as we gather together to celebrate the life of your beautiful child Carole. Please allow her love and spirit to fill our hearts with joy. Amen.

"Thank you all for coming here. I hope that today you will know Carole a little better as a creative artist, friend, sister, courageous fighter of the truth, spiritual inspiration, wife and partner. And my hope is when you leave, a piece of Carole will leave with you, to inspire you to live your own lives as nobly and fully as she did.

"To everything there is a season, and a time to every purpose under heaven.

"Of all the different ways that you could know Carole, the one that stands out the most for me was that Carole was a spiritual warrior. She was born in 1965. I know very little about her early years because thankfully, Carole could not remember it all. She grew up through a very abusive childhood, but that is not how she would want to be remembered. Her struggle only punctuates her success. The darkness in her life allowed her to see the light and rejoice in God's love.

"One of Carole's favorite books was *Be Here Now* by Ram Dass-- a philosophy that Carole adopted-- to live in the moment. All the pain from the past and desperate hope for the future was never as important as what was happening right this instant- 'The Holy Instant.' Every single moment that we live we have a choice to either choose God or not. Anytime you choose God it is peace, bliss, truth, love-- anytime you don't choose God there is pain and suffering.

"A quote from *Be Here Now* that she earmarked reads as follows:

"*'And as Jesus said, 'He who hath ears, let him hear.'*

"*There's something that pulls a person toward this journey. Way, way back deep inside is a memory. There is something deep inside each of us that comes from behind that veil, behind the place of our own birth. It's as if something, somewhere in your past, that's been so high, so much light, so much energy, that nothing you can experience through any of your senses or your thoughts can be enough!*

"'Everybody knows that there is a place which is totally fulfilling. Not a desperate flick of fulfillment. It is a state of fulfillment! You may experience despair that you'll ever know that. Good! Because through despair comes surrender, and through that surrender you come closer to it.

"Please join me if you like:

"The Lord is my shepherd...I shall not want...

"Carole and I knew almost immediately that we were Soul mates.

"We met on St. Patrick's Day, 1992 in a New York subway station. Both of us were waiting to return home to Hoboken. I remember the night clearly, the moment I saw her I knew I had to meet this girl. I asked her if this was the right train to Hoboken, explaining that I had just moved and wasn't sure. Well I kind of knew but she assured me I was going the right way. I introduced myself and she gave me her card .There was a picture of her on it. I insisted on walking her home and she politely shook my hand goodnight. I was on cloud nine. The next day I quickly got out her card and found out I wasn't dreaming. I got up the nerve to call her and she remembered me but declined my offer to dinner saying that she just broke up with someone and wasn't interested. I hung up dejected but after my friend convinced me not to give up I went out in a terrible snow storm, hand-picked the biggest bouquet of flowers and tried again. This time she said yes.

"Literally from our first date we fell madly in love, each asking the other 'where have you been?' Once together, it was years before we even spent just one day apart. Carole is my Soul mate and I will forever be connected to her, forever in love.

"In the end Carole lived in love. She even learned forgiveness and unconditional love of those who hurt her the most. One message Carole would want all of you to leave with is "Choose Love, Not Fear."

"The reason I have asked all of you to come to Spring Lake is because Carole's favorite place was the ocean and this was her favorite beach. It is where we both spent our first summer together, right out there. Our new love burned so brightly that it seemed all we saw was each other yet it felt timeless and everlasting. I am grateful to God and would trade lifetimes for the seven years, five months and fourteen days we were together. I have never been so happy. I have never been so loved.

"Many of you here know Carole as a friend. She was caring, giving and a hell of a lot of fun to be with. She always had a great sense of humor and best of all-- thought I was funny. She used to laugh even when she was mad at me.

"Carole was a loyal friend, always there trying to find the best in people. I've asked Carole's friend of almost twenty years, Julie O'Neal to speak about Carole as a friend.

Julie stood and said, "I met Carole 17 years ago and our friendship clicked in the blink of an eye. We met at a time when we were experimenting with new activities, exploring the mysteries of life and discovering who we were. We were finding out who was fascinating-- or not and what was funny or boring.

"Naturally, we discovered getting into trouble was much more fascinating. Like the time Carole put bubble bath into a hot tub or when we got reprimanded by our group leader in front of the Louvre Museum in Paris for ditching our group.

"Carole and I traveled quite a bit and were able to find fun everywhere we went. We experienced many of the great obstacles in life... school, travel, relationships, careers, and changes of address. All the things you need a good friend to help you through.

"I've been describing Carole to many people these last few days. There's a quote from Kassia- 'You meet your friend, your face brightens, you have struck gold.'

"Carole brightened the room when she walked in -- being in her presence made you feel better even if you thought you already felt great.

"Carole was honest. She always shared what was going on in her mind and heart. Everything she said was always real.

"Carole was loyal. She would stand by you no matter what. She would defend you even when you couldn't defend yourself.

"Carole was sweet, innocent, funny, generous, nurturing, and goofy--- one of my favorite qualities and probably why I like Alex so much.

"Most of all Carole was brave. '*A couer Vaillant rien d'impossible*' -- nothing is impossible to a valiant heart! (Jeanne D'albert)"

Alex continued, "Carole was also a creative force. An award winning painter, lifelong poet, Carole learned to express herself creatively in many ways. She was not only a partner in my life but a partner in work.

"Carole was in sales and sought something more in her professional life. She was fascinated with the film and television industry that I was working in and I encouraged her to follow her dreams. She methodically examined the many jobs in production and then made up her mind she wanted to be a film editor. I had never seen someone make up their mind and commit themselves so successfully to the craft of film making as Carole. On her own she took a weekend training course in Avid editing and then boldly quit a successful career in sales to make minimum wage as an assistant at Pi Editorial, starting from ground zero. Quickly she absorbed skills and knowledge and fearlessly dove into editing. Together we formed a company in 1993 called 'Celestial Productions.' Her artistic abilities catapulted her forward faster than anyone I've ever seen. I would like to play for you Carole's reel which will give you a sample of the kind of work she did and how far she had come."

We then saw Carole's Editorial Reel which I had seen before and loved.

Next, Pete Demas-- the Vice President of MTV Home Video was introduced and told us about Carole's talent and their friendship. They started off working on a documentary called *Straight Dope* and continued working together throughout her career. Pete gave us a perspective on Carole as a professional artist and editor.

Alex continued saying "In her career Carole not only was an award wining editor, but also donated her time for free causes she thought worthy. She loved Mother Theresa and was in awe of this modern saint. Two years ago a woman photographer who lived and worked with Mother Theresa approached Carole to donate time editing a tribute to Mother Theresa. Carole quickly agreed wanting nothing in return. The following is their work which was presented to raise funds for a full length documentary."

We saw the three minute film. Carole's ability to edit was especially masterful in this piece because of how short it was and how much emotional material she worked in with the lyrics of a song called, *She Loved Jesus.* This was not an isolated case of 'high creativity' for Carole. I had seen mostly all of her work and each piece, unique in its own way, showed the same high quality. It was her usual special way of doing things. Once she got into something, anything-- not just editing, she did it with her inspired talent and excellence.

Alex continued, "Carole not only loved the sisters of charity, but was one. Carole disconnected from her entire family (except her sister and her children), because they refused to face the truth of their actions. Carole worked tirelessly to help her sister in her own tribulations. Providing love, well researched advice, money, just about anything to help her and her children. She even told her story to the United States Congress to help her and others in her situation. Most importantly Carole fearlessly supported the truth taking on anyone who tried to deny it from her. After living in lies for so many years, the truth was a precious commodity for Carole. In all the time I knew Carole I can never remember her telling even one lie. I was amazed-- not even one. I've asked Carole sister to give some perspective on Carole as a sister.

Carole's sister spoke tenderly. She read a poem. She expressed all of her love for Carole and even though her body trembled at times-- she didn't need to stop. She moved through her message with love and dignity. It was obvious by her strength that she and Carole were sisters.

Alex said, "Carole lived life to the fullest, courageously taking on each new challenge. She was fearless and loved to have fun. Here is an example of Carole throwing caution to the wind... literally.

Alex showed a video of Carole skydiving. We watched her jump out of a plane and then the camera followed her down.

"Carole not only had courage to fly but even harder she had the courage to heal. She always sought the best in herself and in others. No matter what the cause Carole always reached for the stars. In searching for her own answers Carole came across Eileen King and Sherry Quirk of *One Voice-- The American Coalition for Abuse Awareness--*[and *Justice For Children*.] They give selflessly of themselves helping people around the country and the world.

"Carole was an activist. She felt if she couldn't change others she could change herself and took it on with zeal. I've asked that anyone interested in expressing their sympathies to provide a donation to One Voice because that would honor Carole's life. She was a fighter and believed that even one woman could change the world. After all one man did.

"One Voice introduced us to the best selling author of *Healing The Child Within* and one of the country's top experts on memory and abuse, Dr. Charles Whitfield and his very special wife, author of *Spiritual Awakenings* and *Full Circle* Barbara Harris Whitfield. Coincidentally, they lived in Atlanta and were fighting the same fight. Charlie was immediately Carole's hero and eventually became her teacher, friend and finally the father she never had. I've asked Charlie to talk to you today about Carole's courage to heal and to read from one of the many spiritual books that inspired Carole."

Charlie stood and said, "Thank you, Alex. I am honored that you invited me to talk about Carole. I'm surprised to hear that I was her hero and 'the father she never had.' I didn't know she felt that way.

"I know that Carole was more spiritually aware than most people. I remember that one of her favorite spiritual sources was the modern holy book called *A Course in Miracles*. She and Alex had come to a few of our evening education and discussion sessions that Barbara and I gave on The Course.

"I would like to read you just a sample from The Course that I think Carole identified with. This is from lesson 182 in the workbook of The Course which describes how we are all foreigners to this planet and that our real Source is "God." As Charlie read-- tears came to his and others eyes.

"The title is 'I will be still an instant and go home.'

"This world you seem to live in is not home to you. And somewhere in your mind you know that this is true. A memory of home keeps haunting you, as if there were a place that called you to return, although you do not recognize the voice nor what it is the voice reminds you of. Yet still you feel an alien here, from somewhere all unknown...

"...Some try to put by their suffering in games they play to occupy their time, and keep their sadness from them. Others will deny that they are sad, and do not recognize their tears at all. Still others will maintain that what we speak of is illusion...Yet who, in simple honesty, without defensiveness and self -deception, would deny he understands the words we speak?

"We speak today for everyone who walks this world... A thousand homes he makes, yet none contents his restless mind. He does not understand he builds in vain. The home he seeks can not be made by him. There is no substitute for Heaven...

"Perhaps you think it is your childhood home that you would find again... There is a Child in you who seeks His Father's house, and knows that He is alien here. This childhood is eternal, with an innocence that will endure forever...

"It is this Child in you your Father knows as His Own Son. It is this Child Who knows His Father. He desires to go home so deeply, so unceasingly, His voice cries unto you to let Him rest a while... Give Him just a little time to be Himself...

"This Child needs your protection. He is far from home. He is so little that He seems so easily shut out...

"This Child is your defenselessness; your strength...

"Rest with Him frequently today. For He was willing to become a little Child that you might learn of Him how strong is he who comes without defenses, offering only love's messages to those who think he is their enemy.

"Christ is reborn as but a little Child each time a wanderer would leave his home... This Child...comes defenseless and....protected by defenselessness. Go home with Him from time to time today. You are as much an alien here as He...

"The holy Child remains with you. His home is yours. Today He gives you His defenselessness, and you accept it in exchange for all the toys of battle you have made...

Be still an instant and go home with Him, and be at peace a while."

There was a long pause and then Charlie sat down.

Alex continued, "As Charlie was 'the father Carole never had', Barbara was 'the mother she always wanted.' If Charlie was her hero, Barbara was her savior. Barbara introduced Carole to Spirit-- an expanded view of God and how she could connect directly with it. Carole worked every day-- praying, meditating, reading spiritual literature, creating, working in the garden, anything she could do to connect to the Divine Creative Spirit that also dwelled within her. Barbara showed her some more of the way, step by step. I watched her grow each day and did what I could to try and keep up but never came close. Carole actively sought God's love and then gave it to others freely.   Carole had well developed psychic abilities, a knowing and a connection to the divine and the angels that guided and watched over her connection to God saved her life and opened her to a world beyond our imaginations.

.   I've asked Barbara to talk to you about Carole's spiritual path and where it led to even in her death.

Then I stood up although my legs didn't feel like they were mine. I walked to where Alex was standing and said, "Thank you Alex. The next video is from a television show that Carole and I did. The producer had told me that the youth of Canada were going through hard times. Anti-depressant prescriptions were being given out at an all time high rate to the age group his show caters to--15 to 35 year olds. He hoped that knowledge of the near-death experience could help. When he invited me to Toronto to be on his show, he asked me to bring along another near-death experiencer. So Carole came along and this is the first time she is in front of the camera telling her near-death experience.

Alex reminded me and I said to all these people who had come to honor Carole, "Oh yeah, and she didn't like her hair. She had it cut the day before and she wasn't happy with the way she looked. Also, our flight was late and we didn't get a chance to clean up and change." I was smiling and several people were laughing, so I said, "Well, she would *want* me to tell you!" And we all laughed.

We ran the segment of Carole on Camilla Scott Show. I jumped when she said that she wasn't afraid to die.

When the segment ended, I said, "Carole and I did this television talk show in Toronto in December 1997. I was finishing my third book which is a collection of stories of people I had been with as they died. My editor asked me to tell my near-death experience again for the first chapter so the reader would get some background on my way of helping people. You see, as we just heard Carole say-- near-death experiencers are not afraid to die so it's easier for us to help other people die. Carole helped me write what I am about to read to you from my book.

"I told Carole I was trying to figure out how I could explain what had surged through me and held me. My sense was that Carole too was trying to express her experience with God. This comes from my book, but these words are from Carole and me."

And I read the three pages I had just read twice-- three hours earlier in the car. The words easily flowed from my mouth. I felt I had been taken over-- by my connection with Carole, in which I could feel her reading it with me. I could even see and feel us back in her living room-- I saw the candles she had lit--we were in the center of a circle of candles -- she and I each curled up on the sofa--me with the manuscript in my hands, writing everything she was saying about how she felt -- being with God -- and then me reading it all back to her. I could see her on the other sofa on her knees, sort of jumping and waving her arms and cheering: "We got It! We got it!"

There was more energy coming through me than I ever remembered before while speaking in front of a group. Everyone's eyes were glued to my face. I looked at their faces and occasionally the Atlantic Ocean behind them, reminding me that at the end of the memorial service, Alex was taking Carole's ashes there to join with eternity. As my words were flowing to the faces looking at me, I was also somehow hearing or sensing in my heart that we are all in eternity-- all the time. Our existence appears to be beginning and ending in a linear fashion but that is an illusion. We were who we are before conception or birth and we exist after our death. Experiencing eternity lets us know -- we are more than this blink of an eye we call our life...

Alex then read a letter he had received just the night before from Eileen King. Eileen quoted Carole in the letter so we could hear her again. Alex read,

"'On July 11, 1999 Carole wrote me:

'As far as the documentary is concerned, I really wanted to help people through this process, the way I think I can help people best is to show them how to get their Soul back so it has evolved into a show called "Our Natural Soul." We are currently in the process of editing it-- it is a group of M.D.s and Ph.D.s talking about what our Soul is and how to connect with it. People have told us it is transforming!"

Eileen went on to say, "There are many different warriors among us. I believe that Carole was (and is still) a 'Warrior of Transformation'-- she worked so hard to 'get her Soul back' and was willing to share with others what she had come to know about awakening the forces of the Soul.

"'I know that she will continue to help each of us to awake to our own Soul-- and to the Soul of the other human beings before us. I believe that we can rely on her strong and loving presence and help for the future. Even now, when one turns to her in thought, peace and light-filled joy radiate from her.'"

Alex continued, "Carole's work started as an effort to expose the darkness of abuse but discovered soon that uncovering lies and deceit was far less productive than showing the way to truth. As someone once said, 'She drew the bigger line'. She took the higher road. For Carole truth only came from God and in that truth she found herself. She found happiness and dreamed of spreading this message around the world. I share that dream and through surrendering to God in this tragedy, find divine purpose for my own life.

"Carole was in such a hurry to heal because she wanted to be a mother and start a family -- a chance for her to right the wrongs. We used to say we were going to create our own dynasty, free of pain, anguish and suffering. We made the decision almost a year ago to get ready just as we began shooting seventeen hours of interviews with M.D.s and Ph.D.s at a three day international conference on spirituality. Immediately following she quit a seventeen year smoking habit, began practicing yoga and meditation, and got her life in order. She went through every possession and momento and threw them away unless they were of good memories. Of the eighteen boxes in our attic from her childhood she kept just one. She said she wanted to make room for all the good things to come.

"'Around the end of March we decided we were ready to start trying to have a baby. The timing was precarious because if we got pregnant then the due date would be close to Y2K and the new year. We discussed it and decided that we were not going to start a new Millennium hiding in a corner, trembling in fear. What better way than to bring a life into the world. We were sure that this baby was going to be very important and could change the world. We knew at the very least it would change ours. The very next morning Diane Sawyer, on Good Morning America asked for anyone trying to have the Millennium Baby to write in. Carole did, on a beautiful card with a moon on the front. She wrote: 'we are choosing love not fear.' They invited us to fly immediately to New

York to be on the show with Diane to talk about our decision to try to have 'the Millennium Baby'. We accepted."

Alex ran the tape of the Good Morning America sequence.

"We didn't conceive right away and were disappointed that we weren't going to have the Millennium Baby. We kept trying, but Carole referred to our documentary as 'her baby' and 'if Diane didn't see one she would see the other.'

"Carole worked tirelessly for more that one year first researching-- reading books and information on every speaker-- then forming and asking questions. In each interview, the speaker was looking directly into Carole's eyes and their hearts opened onto the screen. Some were even inspired to speak truths that jeopardized their careers and positions.

"She then dissected seventeen hours of interviews filtering out the best sound bites. After countless hours editing to create a coherent flow, she recently formed the message she wanted to tell. Next she was preparing to add music, images from nature and quotes from every day people about their Soul.

"We eventually got pregnant at the end of May. Carole was ecstatic. Her body bloomed with life and she said she felt a joy she never imagined. Unfortunately, that was short lived. In our sixth week she had bleeding that led us to the doctor's office. Carole had an unusual concern about a tubal pregnancy. We prayed and we saw the fertilized egg in the uterus but the joy was short-lived as well. We were told that it was not a good pregnancy and she would have to get a D&C to end it. She waited, hoped-- but eventually relented. Carole was devastated and the miscarriage hit her very hard.

"After about a month Carole started to feel a little better and we planned a weekend trip to Destin, Florida to heal. When we got there we found out the first two nights we weren't really in Destin, but the next town of Miramar Beach. We laughed-- it didn't seem that we were destined to go to Destin. Carole was complaining of abdominal pains for a couple of days and we went to the emergency room on Sunday. They examined her, x-rayed her abdomen and determined that she had a blockage of severe constipation. I wanted to go home but Carole wanted to finally spend one night in Destin. We ate a seafood dinner, walked on the beach and saw a purple sky at sunset and later that evening she was having more severe pain. After calling the hospital they said they couldn't do anything for her and unfortunately she would have to get through the constipation. The next morning Carole was in great pain, and when I went to call about getting her to the hospital and returned-- she wasn't breathing. I performed mouth to mouth and CPR and got an ambulance there in minutes. They resuscitated her heart and blood pressure. I later found out after three days in a coma and countless tests that she had lost most of her blood internally from a burst tubal pregnancy before the ambulance even arrived.

"Carole was declared brain dead on September 1, 1999. She wanted to donate her organs to help others, and within hours she was finally giving the life she so desperately wanted to.

"Carole's other baby remains with us--her message to the world. Usually you don't show work until it is completed, but I would like to share Carole's legacy with you now. In its final form it will be mixed with music and beautiful scenes of nature. This is a rough cut, but the message is there for you to share. Carole planned to finish this before Thanksgiving and was anxious to get started when we got back from Destin. I hope to carry that out.

Alex turned on the TV and VCR, and the documentary began. I watched the 'man on the street' segment where several people answer the question-- what is Soul? As the documentary continued, I could not connect with it. I was sitting in a sensation of unreality. My reality was shattered and linear time was now divided forever between --before Carole died -- and after. I sunk into a dazed and numb place. As the documentary started to end-- I saw my face on the television screen saying, "Everything we do when we are alive has to do with the entire community of man evolving or falling backwards. We are in the middle of a giant vote right now, whether we're gong to make it as a species or whether we're not. And it's up to each and every one of us."

Bonnie Greenwell says last, "If we had a whole species of people that were allowed to feel wonderful and completely meet their own potential and never saw a barrier in any other human-- We could certainly have a different planet-- couldn't we?"

I remembered Carole saying that after Bonnie's quote she would play John Lennon singing, *Imagine.* I ached for Carole to be there and play the song.

After, people milled around for awhile. We helped pack up the pictures and such. Alex did not pour Carole's ashes into the Atlantic. He said he wasn't ready.

EPILOGUE

SPIRITS IN THE MATERIAL WORLD
CAROLE'S VOICE

My dear friend from Connecticut, Cookie Bruno came to visit us. She explained as I watched her buy food and wine in the super market near our house-- that coming from an Italian family, she wanted to cook for us to help with our grieving. I told her that sounded Jewish and we laughed.

Cookie had never met Carole and Alex. But she felt as though she had known them from all I had told her about them and from watching Good Morning, America. She was meeting Alex that evening because we had invited him and my son, Gary for dinner.

Meanwhile, after we spent time in the kitchen getting dinner going, I sat with Cookie and we watched the Camilla Scott Show-- on near-death experiences.

Then we watched the documentary. I had watched it so many times that I had lost count. However, this time a new theme emerged for me and again the tears rolled down my face. Russ Park's words hit me right in my chest when he said, "Our Soul is something that we cultivate through the challenges in our life. And the way that we do that is through our hearts-- through opening our hearts and having good relationships and taking responsibility for our choices. And really owning those because there is an incredible amount of power in those choices and through that inner life that we all cultivate we learn to open that heart and what we feel and what our authentic self is and that's the miracle of our life."

I heard Yvonne Kason remind me, "We are really spiritual beings having a bodily experience"

Jyoti spoke directly to my pain as she reminded me that, "The thunderstorms are just as beautiful as a sunny day. And so is life."

I saw myself on the screen saying, "God doesn't judge us or know how to judge us. God just loves us."

And finally I heard Russ say, "What I call 'Soul work' is-- when I take something painful and something I am suffering with inside and be with it and be present with it and bring it out and express it in a painting or a song, a poem, whatever that expression might be-- than I take my own suffering and I transform it into something beautiful."

That last quote from Russ planted itself directly into my Soul. It was then that I knew I must write about Carole...I would take my grief and turn it into her story so those who hadn't known her would know her beauty.

I told Cookie many times before about the documentary, but as it finished I saw by the look on her face that she had no idea how impactful it was going to be. She turned to me. Her face was flushed. "I had no idea... No idea at all. I need a copy of this to show my kids. I need to show this to my friends. This is amazing work...

"Oh! Barbara, I'm beginning to understand your loss-- It must be so painful to have lost someone who you could have *this* in common with. You helped them put this together."

"Well," I now knew she understood. I answered with my voice breaking, "We worked together on it. But Alex, and especially Carole, did everything. I invited the speakers and then I chaired the conference that brought them together. Carole worked on the planning of the conference with me. We did all the computer typing and graphics, so we put in a lot of time together. Then when we got the idea that she and Alex could do the documentary, we worked together-- going over all the material that I had and that each speaker sent me. I watched her struggle with the concepts and then I watched her get excited when she figured out what each speaker was about. She explained all this to Alex and sometimes he and I went over it. Often, the four of us spent the evening going over it. It was so stimulating, and hopeful, too-- seeing these two intelligent minds grasp this knowledge.

"They worked really hard at the conference. I saw them only at meal times. They filmed all weekend.

"But the real fun for me began when Carole started editing. I felt overjoyed watching her work. She had an incredible mind to be able to understand and arrange all this material in a coherent understandable message. It was exciting to finally see the documentary's meaning emerge. For so long we weren't sure what the message was going to be, because there was so much information. Then Carole and Alex announced that what we really had was six full hours of theme. This first one we just watched is the pilot. She started sorting out the sound bites for a separate show on healing, understanding energy, addictions and direct connection, and near-death experiences.

"When I watched the first hour emerge-- it gave me so much joy! I sat and watched the monitors over her head as she worked a maze of computer panels. Alex came in after work and brought us dinner. Sometimes we went over and over something to help Carole make up her mind. We worked until one, sometimes two in the morning. I never came home dragging. I always came home exhilarated. I loved the exchanges between Carole and Alex.

I loved to watch the two of them work. They were so good together. They helped each other with their work the same way Charlie and I work together. I loved watching Carole work. I loved her, period and I always will. I just can't get used to her not being here."

Cookie sat quietly. It took her a moment and then she said, "Barbara, she is here with us. I can feel her presence. One of these days you are going to hear her voice in your head. She's here and she will communicate with you. I'm just scared that you are going to be blown away when you hear her. I will pray for you – pray that you will be all right when you hear her."

Cookie went off to call her children and I got the watering can and went out on our deck to take care of the plants. No sooner than I looked up from the pots, out into the forest behind our house and I heard Carole's voice loud and clear. But I wasn't afraid, as I would have been in the past if I heard someone else's voice in my head, and I wasn't emotional either. I loved Carole and I told her so and I told her she could come through anytime. She clearly told me things I would have never expected from her. She told me, "I'm not leaving. I can't leave. I left too many things undone. I'm not happy that I'm here with God because I'm not. I haven't left here. We need to finish what we started."

"How are we going to do it? What do you want me to do?" I asked, feeling some fear and worry.

"I don't want you to worry. Do not worry! I'll take care of it. Just do what is put in front of you. Tell Alex to do the same."

"Yes, Carole. Yes, Honey." Then I finally felt calm, peaceful for the first time since the terrible news. I knew it was really her, not me thinking I heard her because I would have never thought she would say what she said. I went in and found Cookie. I told her what had just happened and that she didn't need to worry. I was all right. I knew I would always miss Carole and I knew I was all right.

A YEAR LATER

And over the next year or so, I began to emerge from my emotional maelstrom. I let myself grieve. I watched Alex grieve. That was painful. We talked often. We continued editing-- following Carole's notes. We churned up every thought, every rationalization, every memory, every fantasy about Carole and her life-- and her death. We looked for meaning. On the first anniversary of her death he poured her ashes into the sea at Spring Lake. We continued to cry together but we also began to laugh.

Charlie helped us when we got stuck in our grief. And we talked for hours with him and sometimes Alex and I talked alone about why Carole had to die at such a young age. Her Soul healed so beautifully. We witnessed it. She transcended her childhood wounds. She released them. She was whole. And Charlie brought us back to the thought that "the body keeps the score." Hers certainly did. She healed her heart, her mind, her Soul-- but her body could not be cured from the severe trauma she had experienced at such a young age and all through her childhood. It looked as though she carried that trauma in every cell of her body. Her body became confused, disoriented and overwhelmed.

We now know from medical research (The ACE Study and others) that child abuse can create all kinds of physical and mental distress as we mature. But we still don't know how to counteract this physical wounding. Perhaps the only way is to stop the abuse -before it starts. And perhaps Carole's millennium baby-- her documentary *Our Natural Soul* will help in the curing of child abuse by helping us learn how to prevent it.

If we awaken to our Souls – we won't abuse our children. That was Carole's wish... that was her hope for all of us--to awaken to our Souls. Her body had to leave but her message-- the wisdom from her experience as she healed herself --her joy--the beauty of her very Soul lives on in this book and continues to live in the life of her baby (her documentary), *"Our Natural Soul."*

—Barbara Harris Whitfield

Atlanta, Georgia
January, 2000

Eleven Years Later

"And over the next year or so, I began to emerge from my emotional maelstrom."

And now, 11 years later as Charlie and I re-read this book and this line above, I look back and I realize that Carole has given us more gifts than I could have ever imagined.

Thank you Carole and God bless you. God certainly blessed us with your presence in our lives.

—Barbara Harris Whitfield

Atlanta, Georgia
January, 2011

APPENDIX I

ACE STUDY SUMMARY 2010

I summarize below a recent book chapter by Vince Felitti and Rob Anda they wrote on the ACE Study findings (Felitti & Anda 2010). For several years I was honored to play a small part by co-authoring seven of the ACE Study's articles and in 1998 writing an editorial commentary for the original publication in the *American Journal of Preventive Medicine*. Below I present a shortened version of their chapter. When the first person plural of *we* and *our* is used it refers to their words, and when I use the first person plural of *I* these are my words.

The Adverse Childhood Experiences (ACE) Study looked carefully at the relationship between repeated childhood trauma and the leading causes of illness, death, and disability in the United States. It found a significant relationship between having a childhood trauma history and later – commonly decades later -- cardiovascular disease, chronic lung disease, chronic liver disease, depression and other forms of mental illness, obesity, smoking, and alcohol and drug abuse. It was, and still is, a major American epidemiological study providing retrospective (a snapshot from the past) and prospective (a series of several snapshots over time – 14 years here) analysis on over 17,000 middle class people of the effect of childhood trauma during the first 18 years of life on adolescent and adult medical and psychiatric disease, sexual behavior, healthcare costs, and life expectancy. It was carried out in Kaiser Permanente's Department of Preventive Medicine in San Diego, in collaboration with the US Centers for Disease Control and Prevention (CDC).

The Study's findings give us remarkable insight into how we become what we are as individuals and as a nation. They are important medically, socially, and economically. Indeed, they have given us reason to reconsider the very structure of medical, public health, and social services practices in America.

The participants were 80% white including Hispanic, 10% black, and 10% Asian; 74% had attended college; their average age was 57. Almost exactly half were men, half women. This is a solidly middle-class group from the 7th largest city in the United States; it is not a group that can be dismissed as atypical, aberrant, or 'not in my practice'.

The study subjects were asked to fill out an 89-item (for men) and 141 (for women) survey regarding several areas of their history and current functioning. They were asked about the following ten kinds of childhood trauma experiences that they may have had, including (with their results in parentheses) :

- Abuse
    1. emotional – recurrent threats, humiliation (11%)
    2. physical—beating, not spanking (28%)
    3. contact sexual abuse (28% women, 16% men; 22% overall)
- Household dysfunction
    1. mother treated violently (13%)
    2. household member was alcoholic or drug user (27%)
    3. household member was imprisoned (6%)
    4. household member was chronically depressed, suicidal, mentally ill, or in psychiatric hospital (17%)
    5. not raised by both biological parents (23%)
- Neglect
    1. physical (10%)
    2. emotional (15%)

We asked them about eight ACEs in the first wave; and added the two categories of neglect in the second wave. The scoring system was simple: the occurrence during childhood or adolescence of any one kind of adverse experience was scored as one point. There was no further scoring for multiple incidents within a category; thus, an alcoholic and a drug user within a household score the same as one alcoholic; multiple sexual molestations by multiple individuals are totaled as one point. If anything, this would tend to understate our findings. The ACE Score can range from 0 to 8 or 10, depending on the data being from Wave 1 or Wave 2.

A third of this middle-class population had an ACE Score of 0. If any one trauma was experienced, there was an 87% likelihood that at least one additional trauma was present. One in six people had an ACE Score of 4 or more, and one in nine scored 5 or more; 59 % scored one or more. Thus, physicians and other clinicians see several high ACE Score patients every day. Typically they are the most difficult ones. Women were 50% more likely than men to have experienced five or more ACEs. We believe that here is a key to what in mainstream epidemiology appears as women's natural proneness to ill-defined health problems such as fibromyalgia, chronic fatigue syndrome, obesity, irritable bowel syndrome, and chronic non-malignant pain syndromes. In light of our findings, we now see these conditions as resulting from medical blindness to social realities and gender.

Somewhat surprisingly, the different ACEs turned out to be about equal to each other in impact; an ACE Score of 4 thus consists of *any* four of them. Here is a sampling from our findings in the ACE Study that show the long-lasting, strongly proportionate, and often profound relationship between ACEs and important categories of emotional state, health risks, disease burden, sexual behavior, disability, and healthcare costs—decades later. We list the health and social problems shown to have a significant graded relationship to the ACE Score in Table 1.

Table1. Health & social problems with a significant, graded relationship to the ACE Score

Type of Problem	*Outcomes Significantly Associated with ACEs*
Medical Diseases	Ischemic heart disease, cancer, including lung cancer, chronic lung disease, skeletal fractures, sexually transmitted diseases, autoimmune diseases, liver disease, and early death; and others not yet published
Risk Factors for Common Diseases/ Poor Health	Smoking, alcohol abuse, promiscuity, obesity, illicit drug use, injected drug use, increased exposure to toxic psychiatric drugs, multiple somatic symptoms, poor self-rated health, high perceived risk of AIDS
Poor Mental Health	Depressive disorders, anxiety, hallucinations, panic reactions, sleep disturbances, memory disturbances, poor anger control, risk of perpetrating or being a victim of domestic violence
Sexual & Reproductive Health	Early age at first intercourse, sexual dissatisfaction, teen pregnancy, unintended pregnancy, teen paternity, fetal death, others not yet published
General Health & Social Problems	High perceived stress, difficulty with job performance, relationship problems, marriage to an alcoholic

To date we have published over 50 scientific articles detailing these findings and presented their related material at over 100 conferences and workshops.

From this remarkable study it is clear that repeated childhood trauma has a profound, proportionate, and long-lasting effect on the victim's current and later emotional states and behavior, whether measured by depression, suicide attempts or other psychiatric symptoms or mental disorders (see Figures 1A, B & C on the next 2 pages). It also has that effect by protective unconscious devices like somatization and dissociation, or by attempts at self-medication ending as high-risk behaviors including drug misuse or addictions that damage the body as medical diseases. Clinicians tend to misguidedly address these high-risk behaviors, addictions or related medical illnesses solely as seemingly simple medical or psychiatric problems rather than dealing with them directly as effects of hidden trauma.

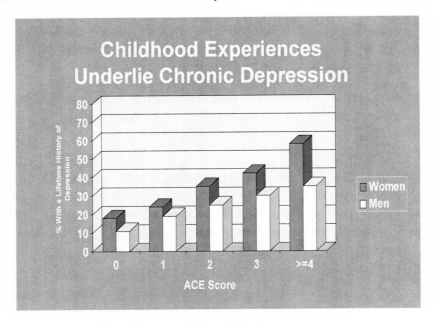

FIGURE 1A – Depression

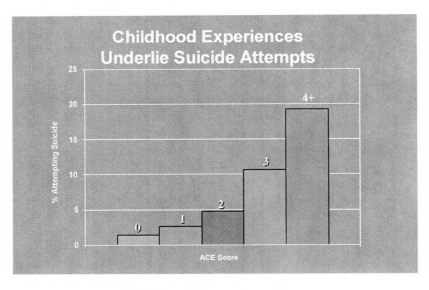

FIGURE 1B – Suicide Attempts

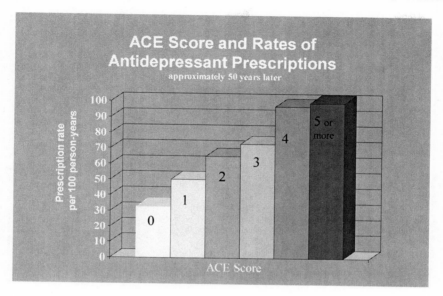

FIGURE 1C – ANTIDEPRESSANT PRESCRIPTIONS

These bar graphs show the strong "stair-step" or graded relationship between childhood trauma and subsequent symptoms, problems or illness. They also show strong, proportionate relationships between the number of ACEs and the use of various psychoactive materials – both illegal and legal drugs -- or other high-risk behaviors (Figures 2A - C). Figure 2 D shows how early trauma significantly relates to later poor self-rated job performance problems.

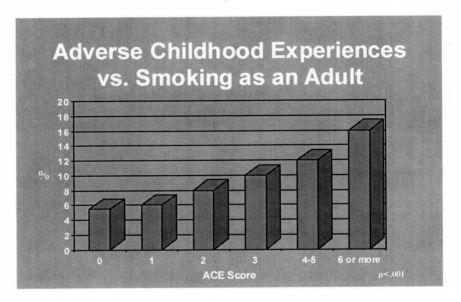

FIGURE 2A – CIGARETTE SMOKING

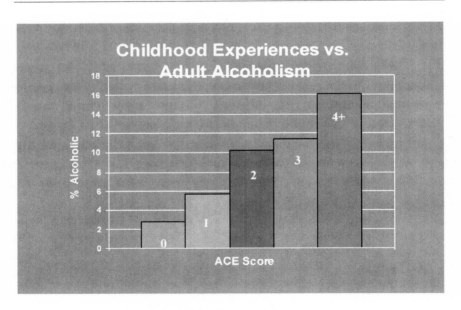

FIGURE 2B – ALCOHOLISM

The ACE Score relationship to IV drug use is particularly striking, given that traumatized boys with an ACE Score 6 or more have a 4,600% increased likelihood of later becoming an injection drug user, compared to boys with a 0 ACE Score. Relationships of this magnitude are rare in epidemiology. Coupled with related information, this finding suggests that the basic cause of IV drug addiction is predominantly trauma experience-dependent during childhood and not substance-dependent. These data have significant implications for medical practice and for treatment programs.

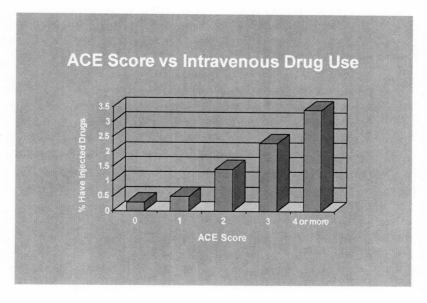

FIGURE 2C - IV DRUG USE

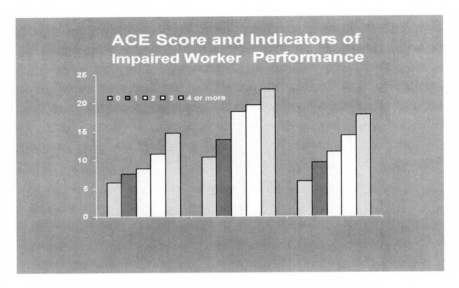

FIGURE 2D - IMPAIRED WORKER PERFORMANCE

Using teen pregnancy and promiscuity as measures of sexual behavior, we found that ACE Score has a proportionate relationship to these outcomes. (Figures 3A & B.) So too does miscarriage of pregnancy, indicating the complexity of the relationship of early trauma to what are usually considered purely biomedical outcomes.

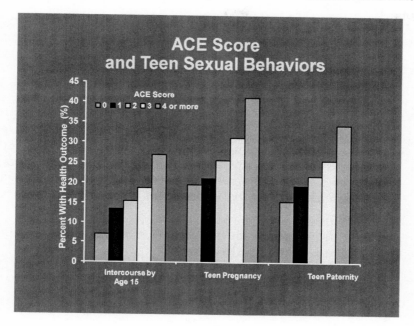

FIGURE 3A - TEEN SEXUAL BEHAVIORS

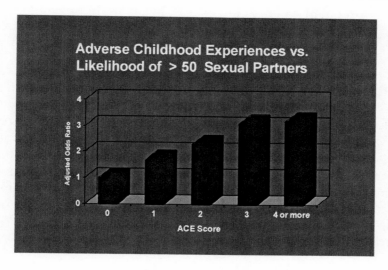

FIGURE 3B – SEXUAL PARTNERS

The total ACE Study data shows that repeated childhood trauma is related to adult disease by at least two basic causal mechanisms:

1) Conventional high risk factors that are attempts at self-medication through the use of drugs like nicotine, alcohol, and other legal and illegal drugs with their many known risks, and

2) The effects of chronic distress through chronic hypercortisolemia, pro-inflammatory cytokines, and other stress responses on the developing brain and body systems, dysregulation of the stress response, and pathophysiological mechanisms yet to be discovered (see PTSD discussion below).

To these two basic causal mechanisms I add the major result of repeated childhood and later trauma:

3) The *lost selfhood* that robs the child and adult's ability to fend for themselves and enjoy life, which I describe in my books (Whitfield 1987, 1990, 1991). The lost self is the real self, our True Self, the core of our being, which I also call the Child Within. This is in contrast to the false self, which we pretend to be in order to survive. From repeated childhood and subsequent trauma our real self goes into hiding and our false self comes up to try to run our life, although it doesn't do that very well -- as most trauma survivors have experienced.

At the core of the trauma lesion is Post-traumatic Stress Disorder (PTSD), which the ACE Study did not look for or address directly. In my extensive research and review of the literature on the effects of childhood trauma as of 2003 I found that *childhood trauma* was significantly associated with and likely *caused most* of the *common mental disorders*, including especially depression and addictions. In Table 2 I show a summary of the large number of peer reviewed published studies that I found that showed a statistically significant relationship between having a history of repeated childhood trauma and subsequent mental illness (Whitfield 2003, 2004).

Table 2. Number of Studies that Document a Significant Link Between Repeated Childhood Trauma and Mental Illness (from Whitfield 2004)

Clinical Area	Clinical	Community	Prospective	Index/Meta Analysis/LitRev	Strength of Data /Total #
Depression	96	70	22	21/2 *	Overwhelming / 327
Suicidality	22	(both)		7	Strong / 29
Alcohol/Drug Probs (SA/CD)	90		21	42 Index, 11 M-A / LitRev	Powerful / 153
Eating Disorders				43 Index, 7 Lit	
PTSD	54	21	10	0/6	Strong / 85
Anxiety Disorder	35	38	12	15/2	Very Strong / 100
Personality Disorders	35			36/1	Very Strong / 76
Psychosis	67		4 (& 2 strong family studies)	37 Index 8 Lit Reviews	Very Strong / 110
ADHD	15		15	4/3	Strong / 77
Aggression & Violence	40		16	10	Strong / 66
Low Self-Esteem	17	10	4	Only 1 of 31 didn't find it	Strong / 31
Dissociative Disorders	30	16	3	11/2	Strong / 57
Nicotine	10		1		Suggestive to Firm / 11
Somatization	38		11	16	Strong / 65
Revicti-mization	38		1	4	Firm to Strong / 38

* Plus Bi-Polar (13), Suicidality (29), and 51 newer-found studies on depression.

At the 14-year mark, we have begun our analysis of the effect of ACEs on adult death rates. This prospective phase of the Study has confirmed that people with ACE Score 6 and higher had a life span almost *two decades shorter* than that of an ACE Score 0 individual of otherwise similar characteristics. But if they work a full recovery program and reduce their risk factors this may lengthen their lifespan and increase its quality and enjoyment.

The treatment implications of the ACE Study are many and large, but the problems of integrating this information into clinical practice are larger. Simply put, it is easier for all of us to deal with the presenting symptom than to attempt to understand it in the full context of the patient, particularly when that full context involves a history of child abuse and household dysfunction that is usually protected by helping professionals' lack of clinical skills, available time, and social taboos against taking a trauma history. Though a direct approach would save time and money in the long run, most physicians and many other clinicians operate in the short run, and address mostly the person's presenting complaints and problems.

These results of the ACE Study may make us uncomfortable. Why would a physician or leader of any major health agency want to leave the familiarity of a traditional biomedical disease approach and enter this area of threatening uncertainty that none of us has been trained to deal with? As physicians, we typically focus our attention on tertiary consequences (presenting symptoms), far downstream, while we protect their primary causes by time, social convention, and taboo. We have thus limited our diagnostic and treatment skills by addressing the smallest part of the problem, that part in which we are comfortable as mere drug prescribers or users of impressive technologies. Thus, although the ACE Study and its fifty-some publications have generated significant intellectual interest in North America and Europe during the past dozen years, its findings are only beginning to be translated into significant clinical or social action. The reasons for this delay are important to consider.

CONCLUSION

The effects of childhood trauma are as dominant as the early trauma psychologists described. They are long-lasting, as though they are sentencing us to a lifetime of pain and confusion -- if we don't heal from them. Even though survivors are prescribed more psychiatric drugs as the ACE study showed above, the drugs don't work well and they are toxic, as others (Breggin 2008, Jackson 2009) and I describe (Whitfield 2003, 2004, 2011).

Many of our most difficult public health problems are the result of compensatory behaviors like smoking, overeating, and alcohol and drug use which provide immediate but only temporary and partial relief from these emotional problems caused by childhood trauma. We usually don't recognize the chronic life distress from the repeated childhood and later trauma as a second causal mechanism for illness. These experiences tend to be lost in time and concealed by our shame, secrecy, and social taboo against the exploration of certain topics of human experience.

The findings of the ACE Study provide a credible basis for a new paradigm of medical, public health, and social service practice that would start with comprehensive biopsychosocial evaluation of all patients at the outset of ongoing medical care. We have demonstrated in our practice that this approach is acceptable to patients, affordable, and beneficial in multiple ways. The potential gain is huge. So too is the likelihood of clinician and institutional resistance to this change. Actualizing the benefits of this paradigm shift will depend on first identifying and resolving the various bases for resisting it. In reality, this will require far more planning than would be needed to introduce a purely intellectual or technical advance. Our experience suggests that we can do it.

Charles L. Whitfield, MD

Atlanta, Georgia
January, 2011

ACE STUDY REFERENCES

Breggin PR (2008) *Brain-Disabling Treatments in Psychiatry: Drugs, electroshock, and the psychopharmacutical complex.* 2nd edition Springer Publishing, NY

Felitti VJ, Anda RF, Nordenberg D, Williamson DF, Spitz AM, Edwards V, Koss MP, Marks JS (1998) The relationship of adult health status to childhood abuse and household dysfunction. *American Journal of Preventive Medicine.* 14: 245–258

Felitti VJ, Anda RF (2010) Chapter 8. The Relationship of Adverse Childhood Experiences to Adult Medical Disease, Psychiatric Disorders, and Sexual Behavior: Implications for healthcare. in R Lanius & E Vermetten eds. *The Hidden Epidemic*: The Impact of Early Life Trauma on Health and Disease. Cambridge University Press

Jackson GE (2009) *Drug-Induced Dementia*: a perfect crime. Author House, Bloomington, IN

Whitfield CL: *The Truth about Depression*: Choices for Healing. Health Communications, Deerfield Beach, FL, 2003 (800-851-9100)

Whitfield CL: *The Truth about Mental Illness*: Choices for Healing. Health Communications, Deerfield Beach, FL, 2004

Whitfield CL (2011) *Not Crazy*: You may NOT be Mentally Ill. Muse House Press, Atlanta

APPENDIX II

These are the lyrics of a song written a short time later for Carole by Kate Hart, also a survivor. She has a sense that she didn't write this song, but that Carole did.

OUR CAROLE'S SONG

I'm in the love.
I am at Peace.
Don't worry about me
'Cause now I'm free
Free to understand the answers
My life and what it means to me.

My Soul mate, my love
All we ever wanted was that
Gift from above.
I'm so sorry I had to leave
In our forever love you must believe.

You wanted to know that I'm all right
And why my body couldn't fight.
But this was all part of our plan
To help us grow, to understand.

You know I knew how peaceful life
Like this could be.
I'm with the Soul of our child
And now we both live free.

I have no fear
I am God
You I will see
Always, we will be.

The sun moon and stars
Seemed to be so far.
Everyone already has what they're
looking for.
It's peace in your heart, your Soul
Your spirit and nothing more.
I am like this song.
I keep going on... And on, And on...

REFERENCES

Van der Kolk BA & Fisler R. Dissociation and the fragmentary nature of traumatic memories: overview and exploratory study. Journal of Traumatic Stress 1995; 8:505-525.

Felitti VJ, Anda RF, Nordenberg D et al. The relationship of adult health status to childhood abuse and household dysfunction. This issue American Journal of Preventive Medicine, April 1998.

Whitfield (Harris) B. Full Circle: The Near-Death Experience and Beyond. Simon and Schuster Pocket. New York NY, 1990

Whitfield B. Spiritual Awakenings: Insights to the NDE and Other Doorways to Our Soul. Deerfield Beach FL: Health Communications, 1995.

Whitfield B. Final Passage: Sharing the Journey as This Life Ends. Deerfield Beach FL: Health Communications, 1998.

Whitfield B., Whitfield B et al. The Power of Humility: Choosing Peace over Conflict in Relationships. Deerfield Beach FL: Health Communications, 2006.

Whitfield B. The Natural Soul: Unity with the Spiritual Energy that Connects us: What It Looks Like and How It Feels. Atlanta GA: Muse House Press, 2010.

Whitfield CL. Memory and Abuse: remembering and healing the wounds of trauma. Deerfield Beach FL: Health Communications, 1995.

Whitfield CL. Traumatic amnesia: the evolution of our understanding from a clinical and legal perspective. Sexual Addiction & Compulsivity 1997a; 4(2): 107-133.

Whitfield CL. Trauma and memory; In A Burgess (ed). Advanced Psychiatric Nursing. NY, Appleton-Lange, 1998.

Whitfield CL. Internal verification and corroboration of traumatic memories of child sexual abuse. Journal of Child Sexual Abuse 1997b; 6:3.

Herman J. Trauma and Recovery. NY: Basic Books 1992. American Psychiatric Association

Rowan AB & Foy DW. PTSD in child sexual abuse. Journal of Traumatic Stress 1993; 6:3-20.

Whitfield CL. Healing the Child Within: discovery and recovery for adult children of dysfunctional families. Deerfield Beach FL: Health Communications, 1987.

Whitfield CL: *The Truth About Depression: Choices in Healing Mental Illness.* Health Communications, Inc. Deerfield Beach, Florida 2003

Whitfield CL: *The Truth about Mental Illness.* Health Communications, Inc. Deerfield Beach, Florida 2004

Whitfield CL: *Not Crazy: You May not Be mentally Ill.* Muse House Press, Atlanta, Georgia 2011

INDEX

ABOUT THE AUTHOR

Barbara H. Whitfield, R.T., C.M.T., is the author of many published articles and five books: *Full Circle: The Near-Death Experience and Beyond, Spiritual Awakenings: Insights of the Near-Death Experience and Other Doorways to Our Soul, Final Passage: Sharing the Journey as This Life Ends, The Natural Soul: Unity with the Spiritual Energy that Connects us* and co-author with Charles Whitfield and Jyoti and Russell Park of *The Power of Humility: Choosing Peace over Conflict in Relationships*. Barbara is a researcher, workshop presenter, Near-Death Experiencer and respiratory and massage therapist.

She was on the faculty of Rutgers University's Institute for Alcohol and Drug Studies for 12 years teaching courses on the after effects of Spiritual awakenings. Barbara was research assistant to psychiatry professor Bruce Greyson, the director of research for the International Association for Near-Death Studies (I.A.N.D.S.) at the University of Connecticut Medical School, studying the Spiritual, psychological, physical and energetic after-effects of the Near-Death Experience. She is past president and a member of the board of the Kundalini Research Network and has sat on the executive board of the I.A.N.D.S. She is a consulting editor and contributor for the Journal of Near-Death Studies.

Barbara was a key subject in Kenneth Ring's groundbreaking book on the Near-Death Experience, *Heading Toward Omega*. He writes about her again in his latest book *Lessons From the Light*.

Barbara has been a guest on major television talk shows, including Larry King Live, A&E's Bio Channel series "Beyond and Back," Alabama Public Television's documentary *Life After Death*, The Today Show, Man Alive, Donahue, Unsolved Mysteries, PM Magazine, Good Morning America, Oprah, Joan Rivers, Sonya

Freeman, and CNN Medical News. Her story and her research have appeared in documentaries in the US, Canada, Japan, France, Belgium and Italy and in magazines such as Redbook, McCalls, Woman's World, McClean's, Utne Reader, Common Boundary, Psychology Today and many others. She presented talks on the Near-Death Experience to a group on Capital Hill in Washington, D.C. and also the United Nations in New York.

Barbara lives in Atlanta, Georgia with her husband, bestselling author and physician Charles Whitfield, MD. They share a private practice where they provide individual and group psychotherapy for trauma survivors and people with addictions and other problems in living.

Find more of Barbara's writings and websites at:

www.MuseHousePress.com

www.BarbaraWhitfield.com

You can write Barbara at:
Barbara-Whitfield.Blogspot.com

MORE BOOKS BY BARBARA AND CHARLES WHITFIELD

"The Natural Soul is a work of art that helps us shift from a fear-based sense of death to one that embraces its nature and opens the door of its Mystery. Barbara's compelling words weave a story of inspiration where the reader will find hope.

It invites the Soul to soar."

—Jyoti (Jeneane Prevatt, PhD), and Russell Park, PhD., Clinical Psychologist, Co-authors of *The Power of Humility*.

More Books by Barbara Harris Whitfield

"This is an important book because it is about transformation of consciousness, using our relationships as our spiritual path."

Sharon K Cormier,
Registered Yoga Teacher
Near-death Experiencer

"Spiritual Awakenings breaks new ground both for Barbara Harris Whitfield and for the field of near-death studies."

Bruce Greyson, M.D.,
Editor The Journal of
Near-Death Studies

www.barbarawhitfield.com

More Books by Barbara Harris Whitfield

"Final Passage should be required reading for heathcare professionals who care for the terminally ill."

Jack McBride,
Executive Director,
Shepherd's Gate
Hospice,
Covington, GA

"Her personal story and her eloquent, lucid and compelling way of competently expressing the difficulties, positive and negative effects of NDErs, and coming to terms with the ND experience in one's life is a priceless gift."

Amazon Reviewer

www.barbarawhitfield.com

Depression hurts. Sometimes it overwhelms. But what do we really know about it? Is the current opinion about its nature and treatment true? Whether you or someone you know suffers from depression, you have choices that will enhance recovery.

Renowned physician, psychotherapist and best-selling author Charles Whitfield MD offers new hope. In The Truth about Depression.

"One in five American adults suffers from some kind of "mental disorder." The Truth About Mental Illness uncovers the myths and realities of disorders such as post-traumatic stress, ADD, anxiety, eating disorders, drug addiction, schizophrenia, and personality disorders. Whitfield offers cutting-edge research into their causes; why the real causes are often overlooked..."
                    —HCI Book Review

Choosing God

A Bird's Eye View of
A Course in Miracles

Charles L. Whitfield, MD
Author of Healing The Child Within
and
The Power of Humility

ᄳᄨP
muse house press

"This book takes over where the Twelve Steps leave off. Charles Whitfield skillfully explains the connections between the Twelve Steps and the spirituality of A Course in Miracles and the growth we can have beyond Twelve Step Work."

—Jack C., Twelve Step Fellowship Member

"Dr. Charles Whitfield is the clearest teacher on A Course in Miracles that I have ever heard. I have always respected and used his work."

—Ken Keyes, Jr. Author of the best-selling Handbook to Higher Consciousness

Teachers of God

Further Reflections on
A Course in Miracles

Charles L Whitfield, MD
Author of Healing The Child Within
and
The Power of Humility

ᄳᄨP
muse house press

If you or someone you know has a diagnosis of any kind of mental illness, this book may help. There is a way out — as described in its 15 compact chapters.

"In my over 30 years assisting countless people with a variety of mental, emotional, behavioral and relationship problems, I have come to realize that many of them have been misdiagnosed and mistreated. In fact, most of them were not mentally ill. In this book I share research and experience and offer hope and another way that may successfully address what may not be a "mental illness."
                                                           —Charles L. Whitfield, MD